The History of
Handspinning in Art

Portrayed in a collection of paintings, drawings,
and prints from Western art between 1500 -1900

by Tulasi Zimmer

The History of
Handspinning in Art
Portrayed in a collection of paintings, drawings,
and prints from Western art between 1500 -1900

Cover Design by: Tulasi Zimmer

Cover painting :
"Lullaby"
by Wilhelm Bouguereau
in the 1875

ISBN-13: 978-0-9892411-4-4
ISBN-10: 0989241149

Printed in U.S.A

CRYSTALMOON
PUBLISHING

INTRODUCTION

Handspinning is the art of twisting fiber into a continuous thread. Traditionally a spinning wheel and/or a drop spindle is used to supply twist to the fiber. The thread is spun thick or thin, plied or un-plied, and can be dyed or left natural. Handspun yarn is very popular today, and is often used for knitting, crochet, weaving, and fiber arts projects.

Before the industrial age, in the Western cultures, handspinning was considered a skilled occupation and essential to the success of the cottage and textile industries. It was also one of the few livelihoods available to women that enabled them to live independently. The women who spun yarn were called "spinsters" and the men were known as "spinners".

My professional career is in fine arts, painting and drawing, and I learned handspinning in 1999. Since then, I have discovered that textile artisans were a very popular subject for artists to paint and draw before the 1900's. Hence, came the idea for creating this book. I chose paintings, drawings, and prints from Western art that I feel help tell the story of life as a handspinner during that era. The images also display equipment and tools associated with handspinning such as; spinning wheels, distaffs, hand spindles, yarn reels, niddy noddys, and /or wool carders.

I hope you enjoy viewing this collection of beautiful art and learning about the history of handspinning fiber into yarn. - Tulasi

The Evolution of Handspinning

Handspinning is still a common practice that can be found in many parts of the world today. The principles of handspinning have remained virtually unchanged during its history.

Drafting and twisting fibers between the palms of the hand was the first method of handspinning, which later evolved into rolling fiber in-between the palm of the hand and the thigh, to form a continuous thread. Eventually a tool, now known as a "drop spindle", consisting primarily of a stick (staff) with a notch at the top and a weight at the bottom, like a rock (whorl), was used. Another stick called a "distaff" was wound with the raw fiber to be spun, which was usually wool or flax (flax was used for making linen). The distaff was carried under the arm or placed in the belt the handspinner. This enabled the handspinner to draft the fiber to be spun with one hand, from the distaff, and twirl the spindle with the other to put twist into the fiber. The spun thread was then wrapped around the staff of the spindle for storage and the process was repeated until the desired length of thread was spun. The hand spindle was primarily used for spinning all the thread and yarn needed for producing fabric until the 15th century.

The hand spindle was eventually superseded by the spinning wheel at the end of the Middle Age. The origin of the spinning wheel is not clearly known, but it can be traced back to the Far East and India. The first known spinning wheel consisted of a spindle and wheel set into a wood frame driven by a band on a pulley. The wheel was operated by the handspinner rotating the wheel with one hand and drafting the fiber from a distaff that was either attached to the wheel or mounted next to it. After spinning a length of thread, the wheel was stopped and rotated in the opposite direction, in order for the yarn to be "hacked off" and wound onto the spindle. By the 17th century, a treadle was added to the wheel. This allowed the spinner to operate the wheel without using their feet, therefore, freeing both hands for an easier manipulation of the fibers. It was then possible to draft, twist, and wind the yarn in one continuous motion, which greatly increased production.

The art that followings illustrates the occupation of handspinning and various tools/equipment used for making yarn before the 1900's. Brief descriptions about the art work and a few additional comments are also added. Last, the images are digitally enhanced to improve the color quality and clarity.

If you would like to learn more about handspinning visit the Joy of Handspinning at www.joyofhandspinning.com.

Paintings

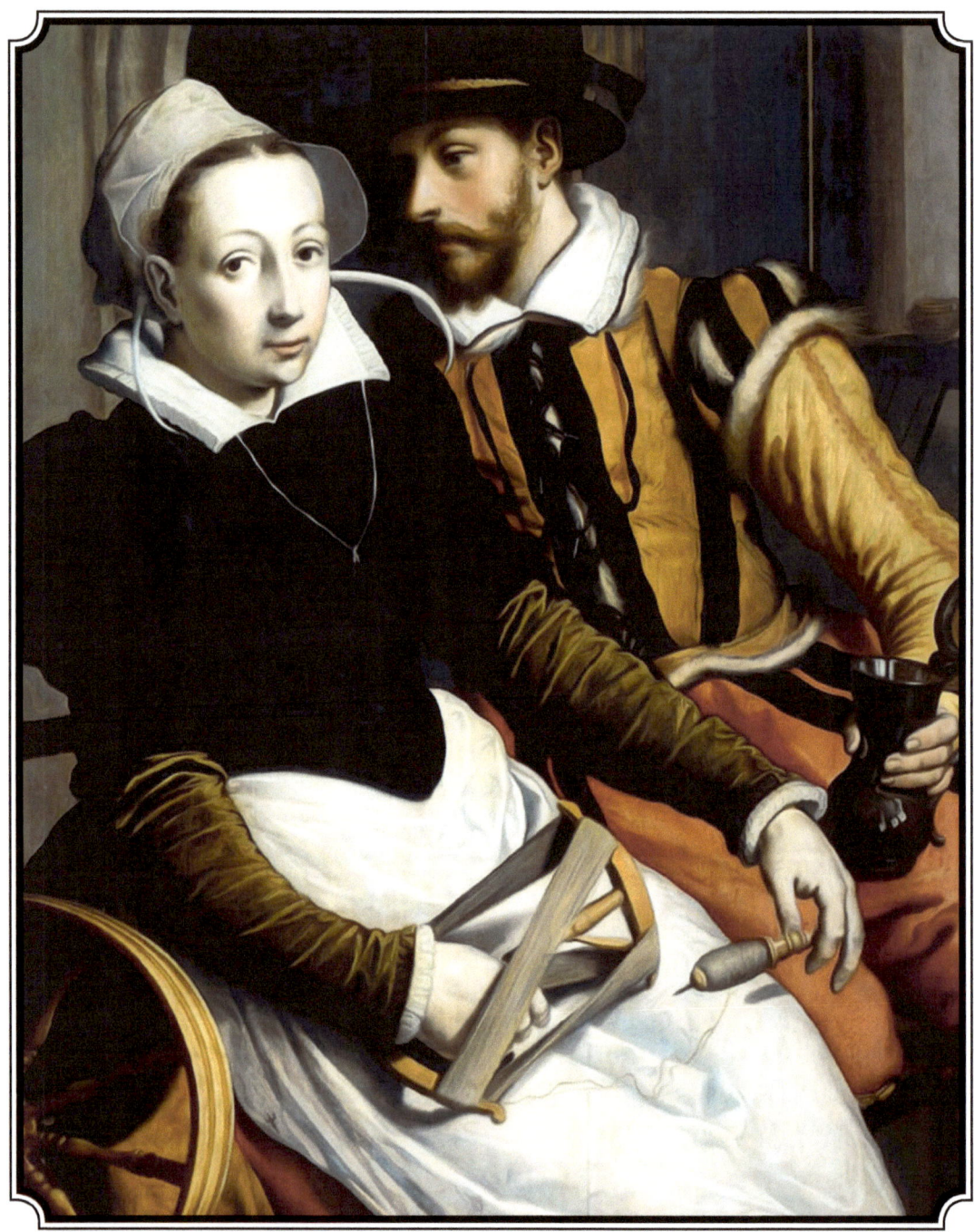

"The Interruption", by Pieter Pietersz
Oil, c.1500s

A spinster seated next to a spinning wheel is winding spun thread from a hand spindle onto a niddy noddy sitting in her lap. A niddy noddy is used to arrange the spun yarn/ thread into a skein.

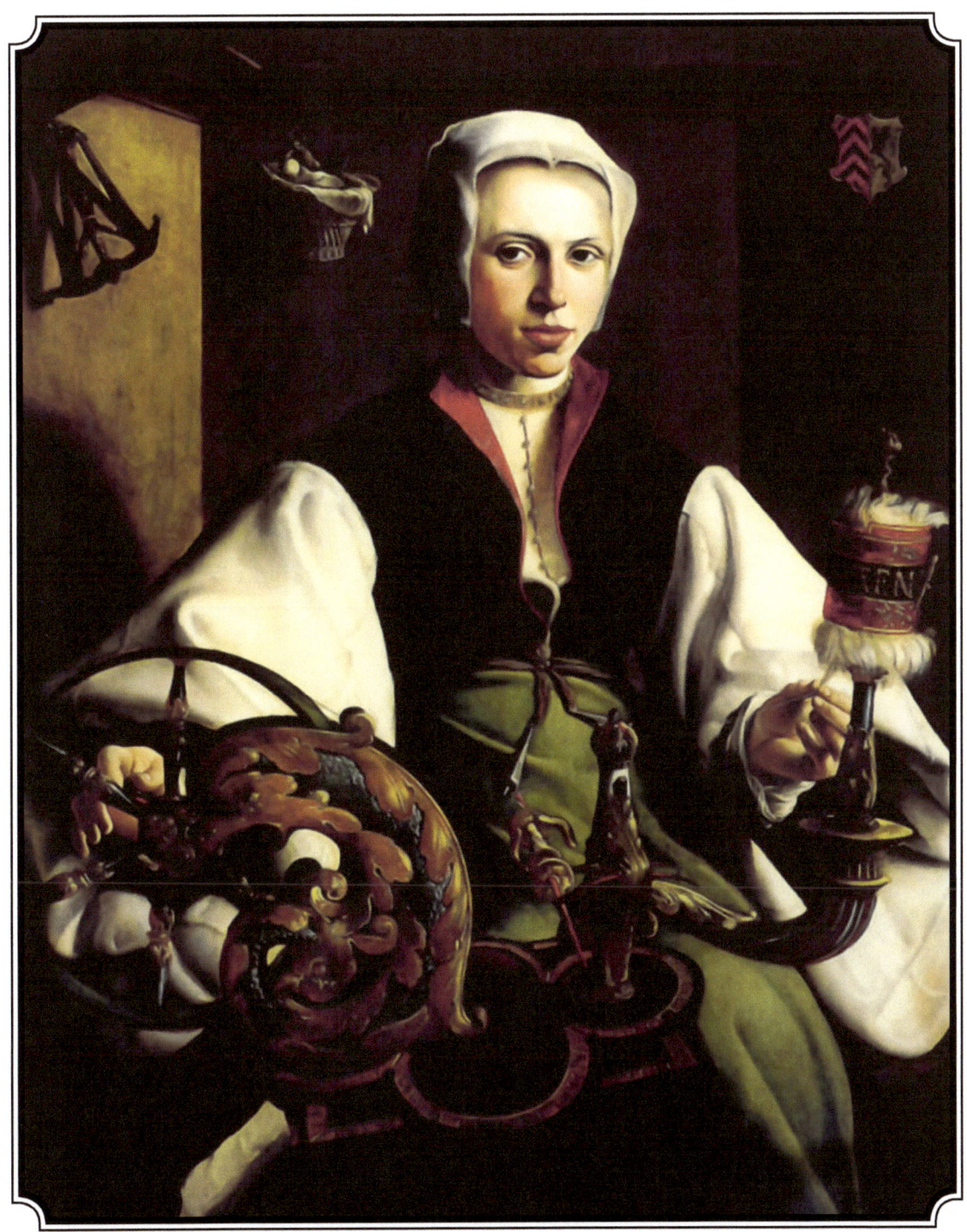

"Portrait of a Woman with Spindle and Distaff", by Maarten Van Heemskerck
Oil, c.1500s

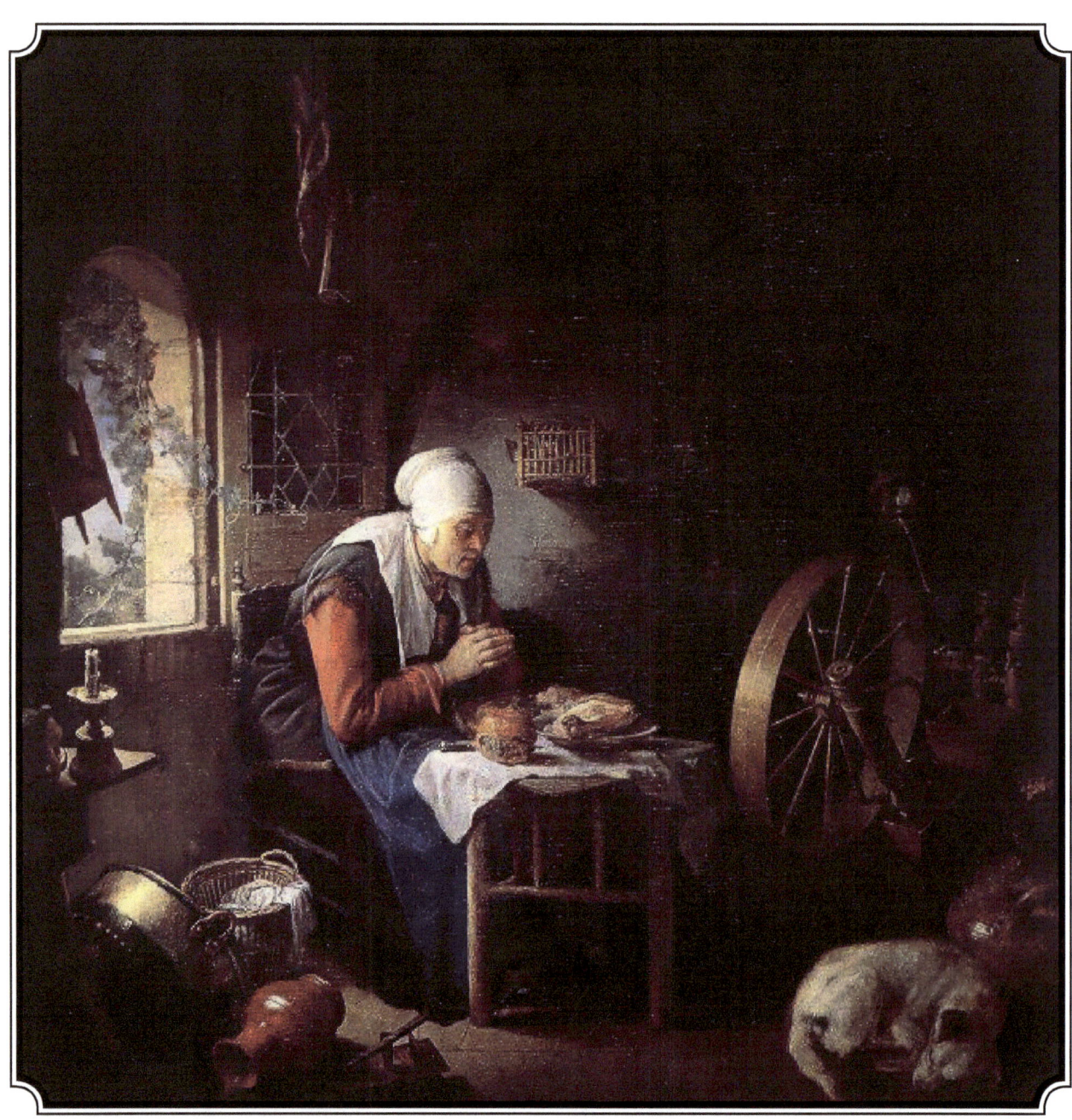

"Prayer of the Spinster", by Gerrit Dou
Oil, c.1600s

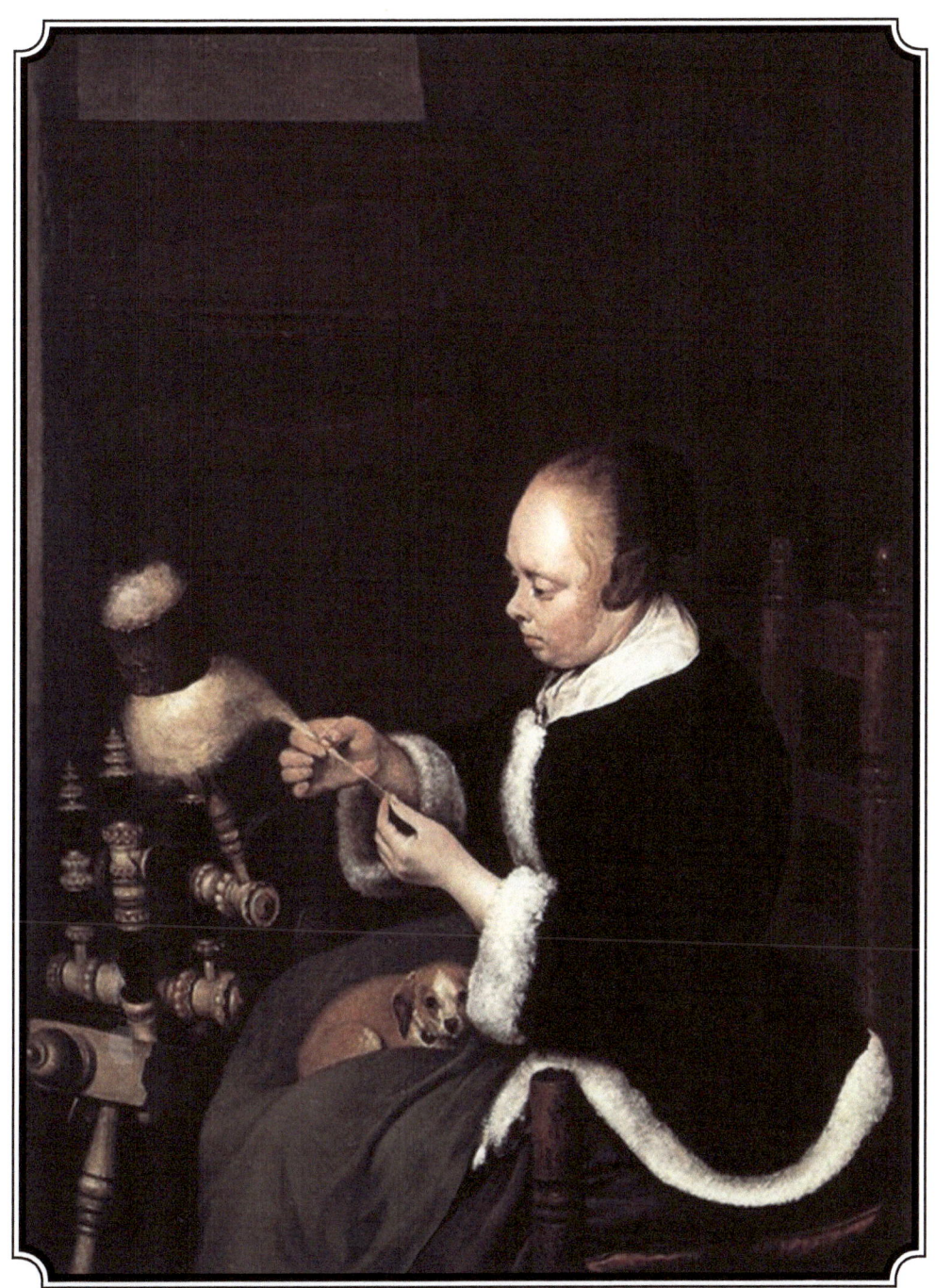

"A Woman Spinning", by Terborch
Oil, c.1600s

A spinster drafting fiber from a distaff
which is mounted on the spinning wheel.

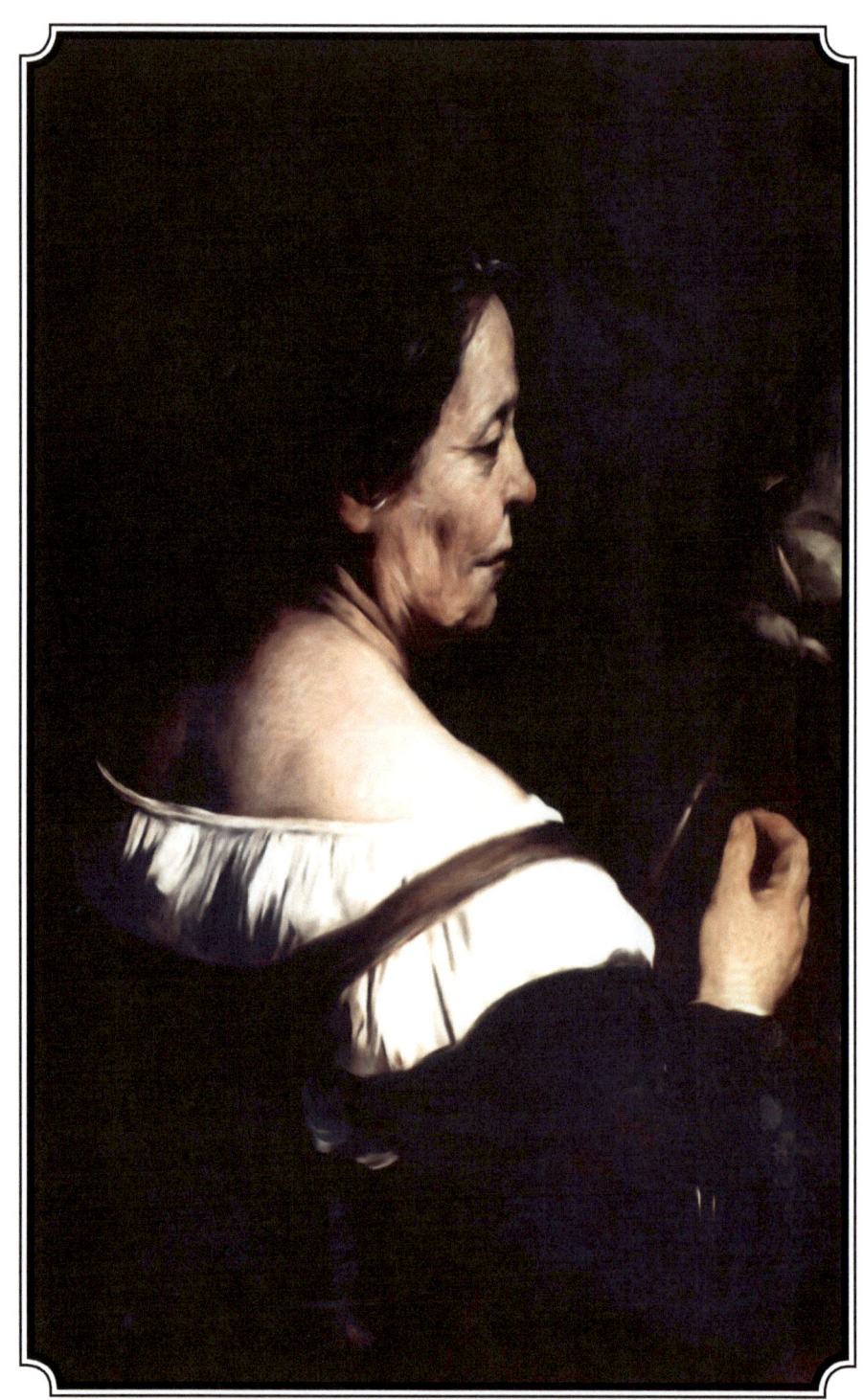

"Old Woman with a Distaff" by Pier Francesco Mola
Oil, 1600s

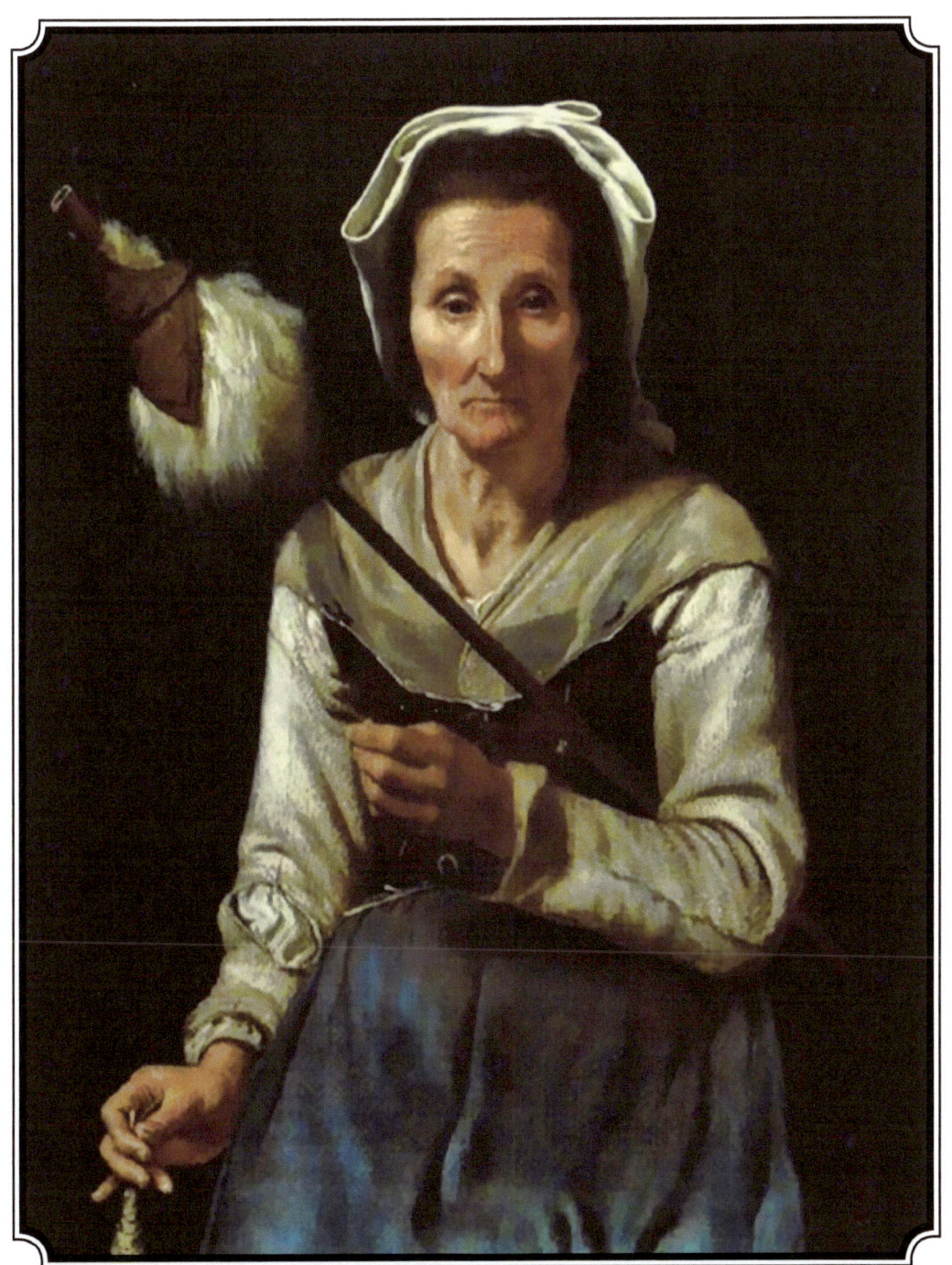

"Old Woman Spinning", by Michael Sweerts
Oil, 1646

This spinster is holding her distaff, full of fiber, under her arm while she twirls the spindle to twist the fiber into yarn.

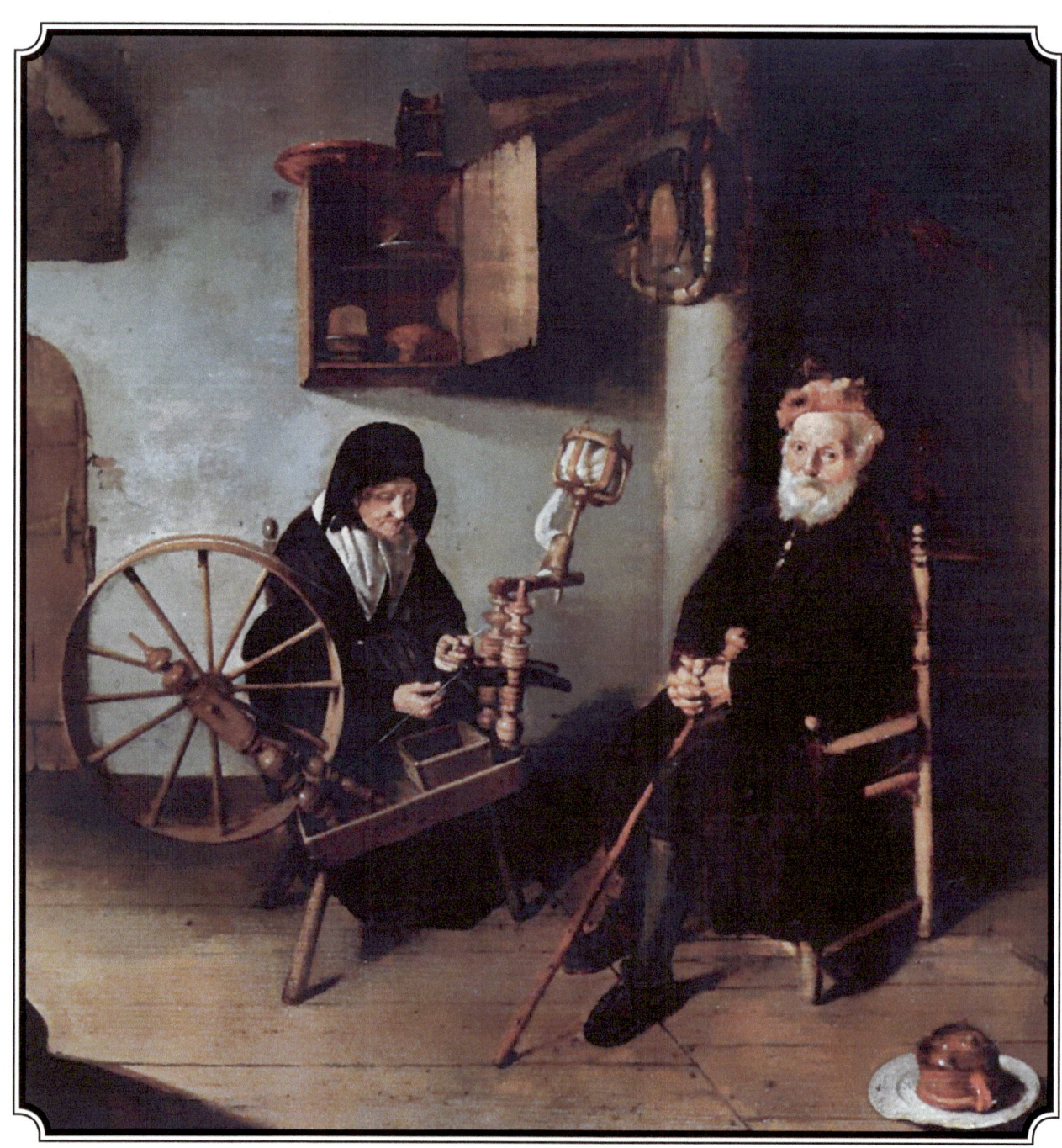

"The Spinster", by Quiringh van Brekelenkam
Oil, 1653

This painting portrays a spinster drafting fiber from a mounted distaff on a Saxony style spinning wheel. The elements of a Saxony wheel are arranged horizontally, with a large wheel at one end; the flyer at the other; and normally has three legs.

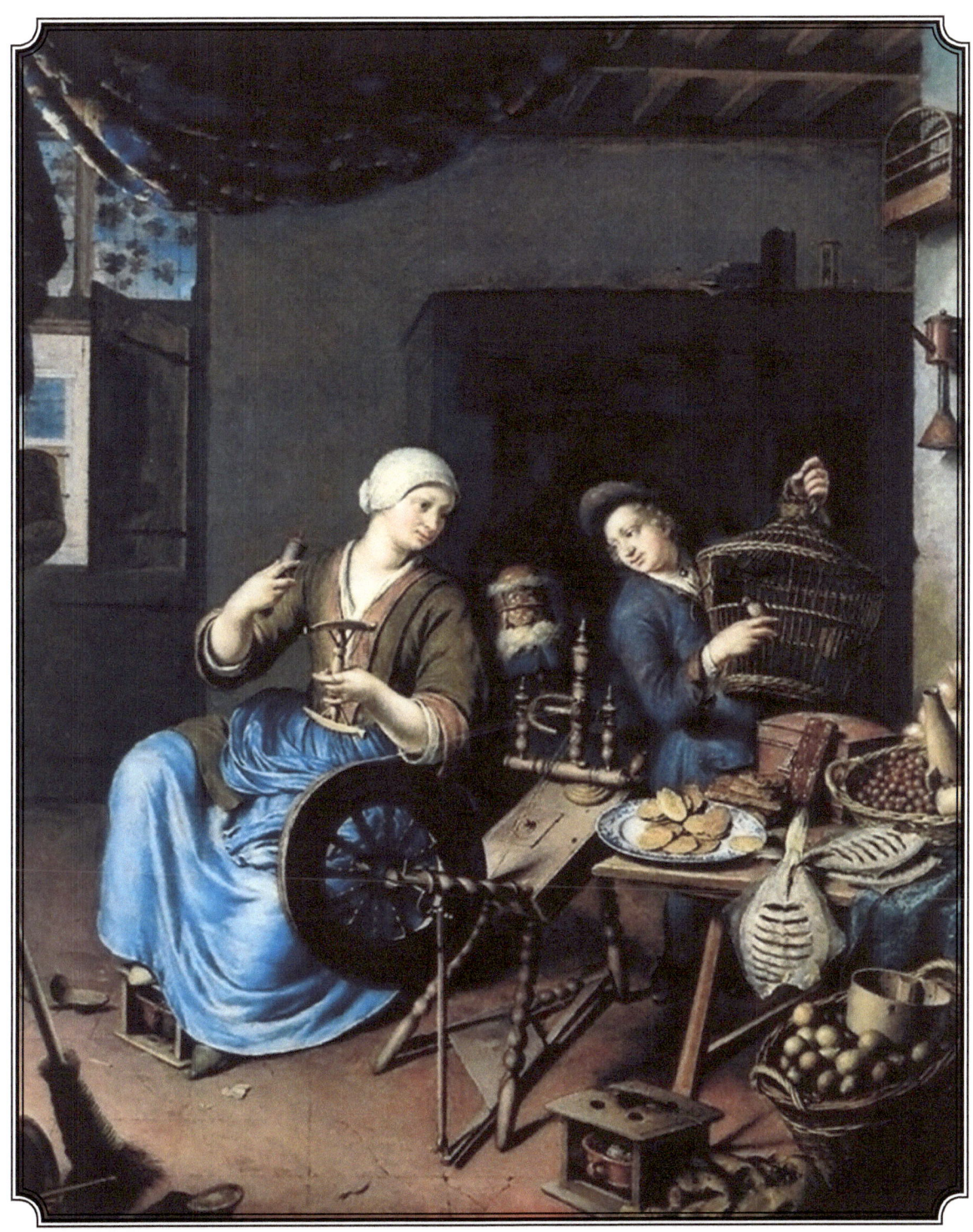

"The Spinster", by Willem Van Mieris
Oil, c.1700s

This painting shows a spinster winding the spun yarn off of the spinning wheel's bobbin and onto a niddy noddy to form a skein of yarn for easy storage and/or dyeing.

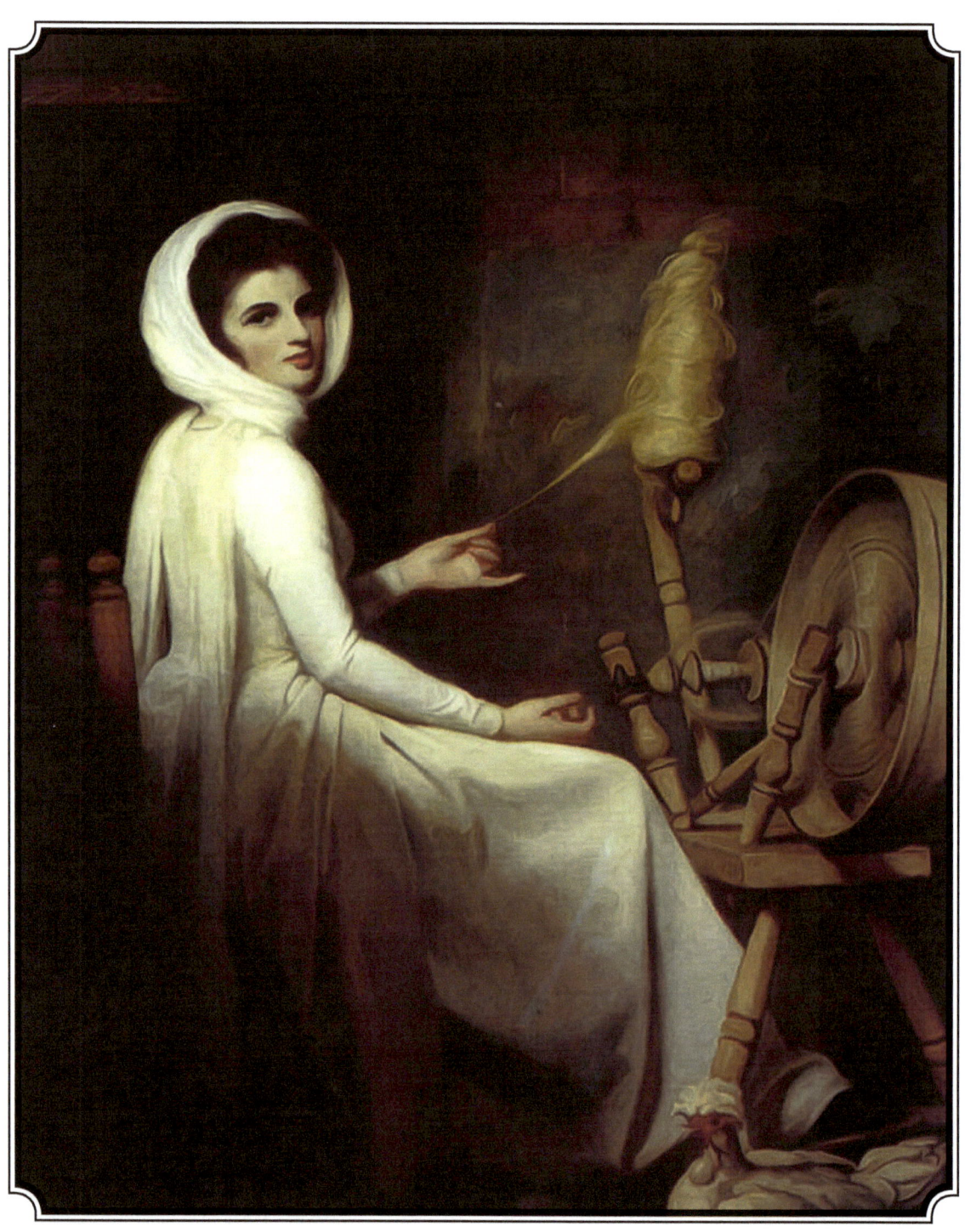

"Lady Hamilton as a Spinner", by George Dalton Romney
Oil, c.1700s

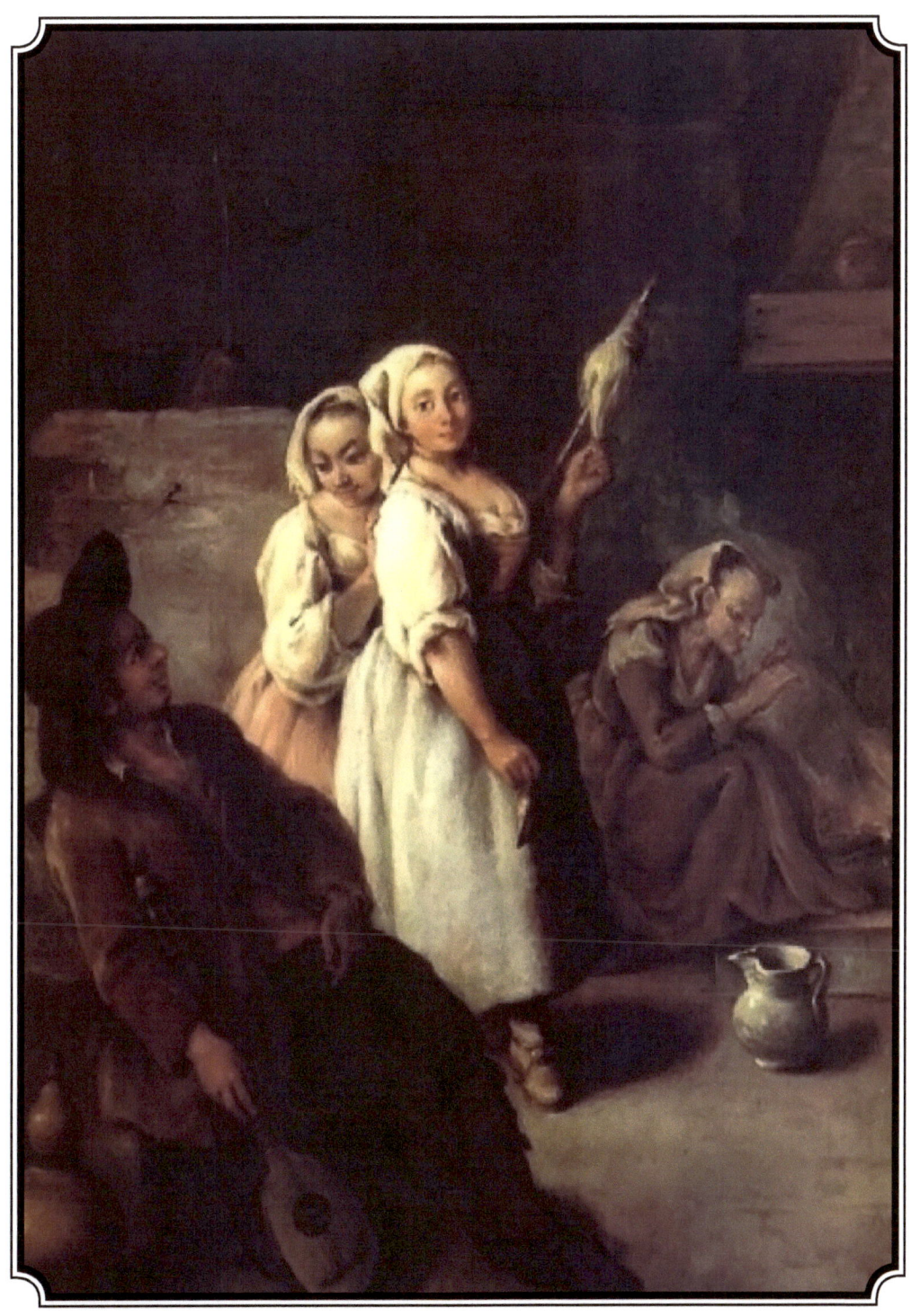

"The Spinster", by Pietro Longhi
Oil, c.1700s

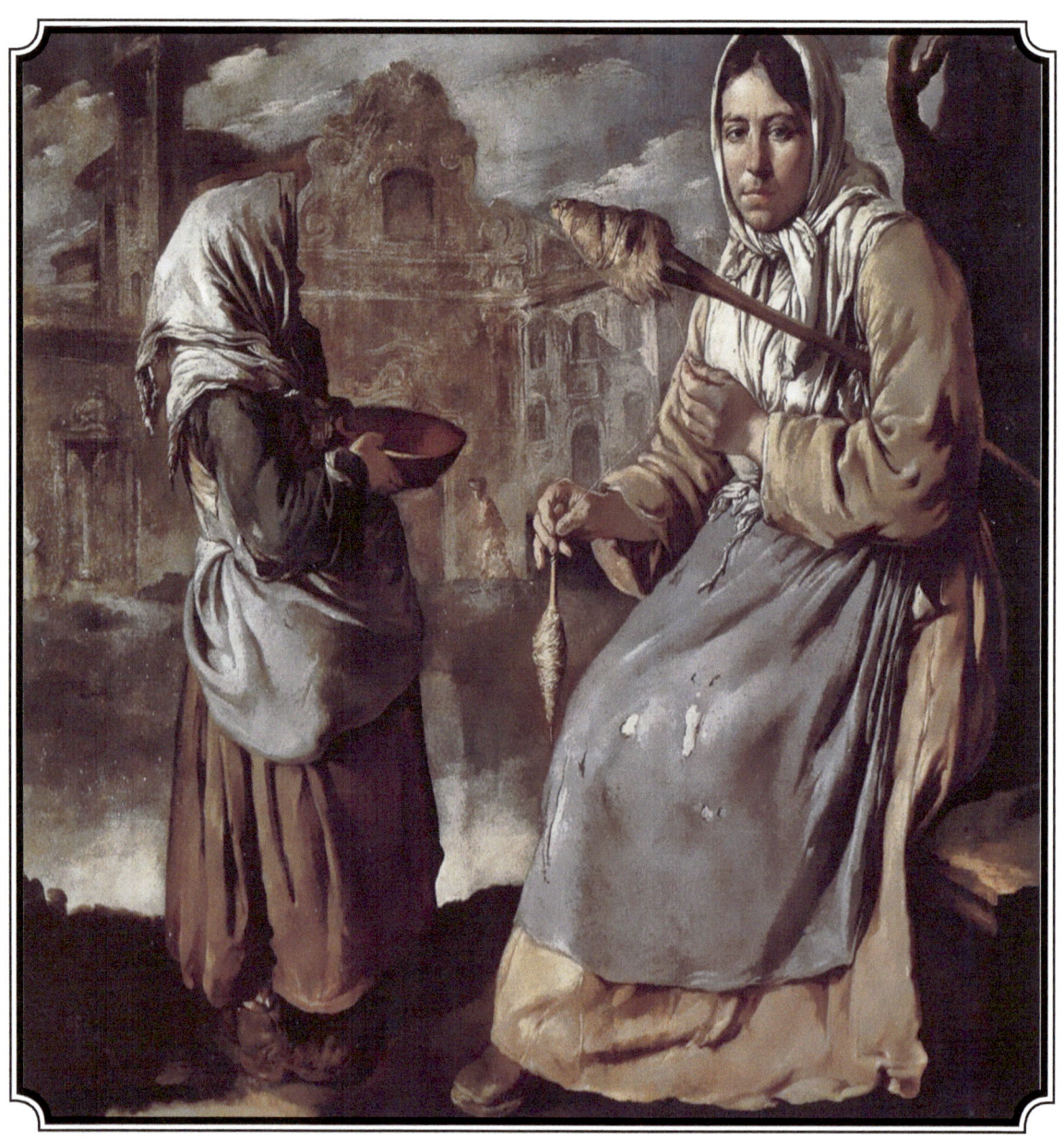

"Begging Girl and Woman Spinning", by Giacomo Ceruti
Oil, 1720

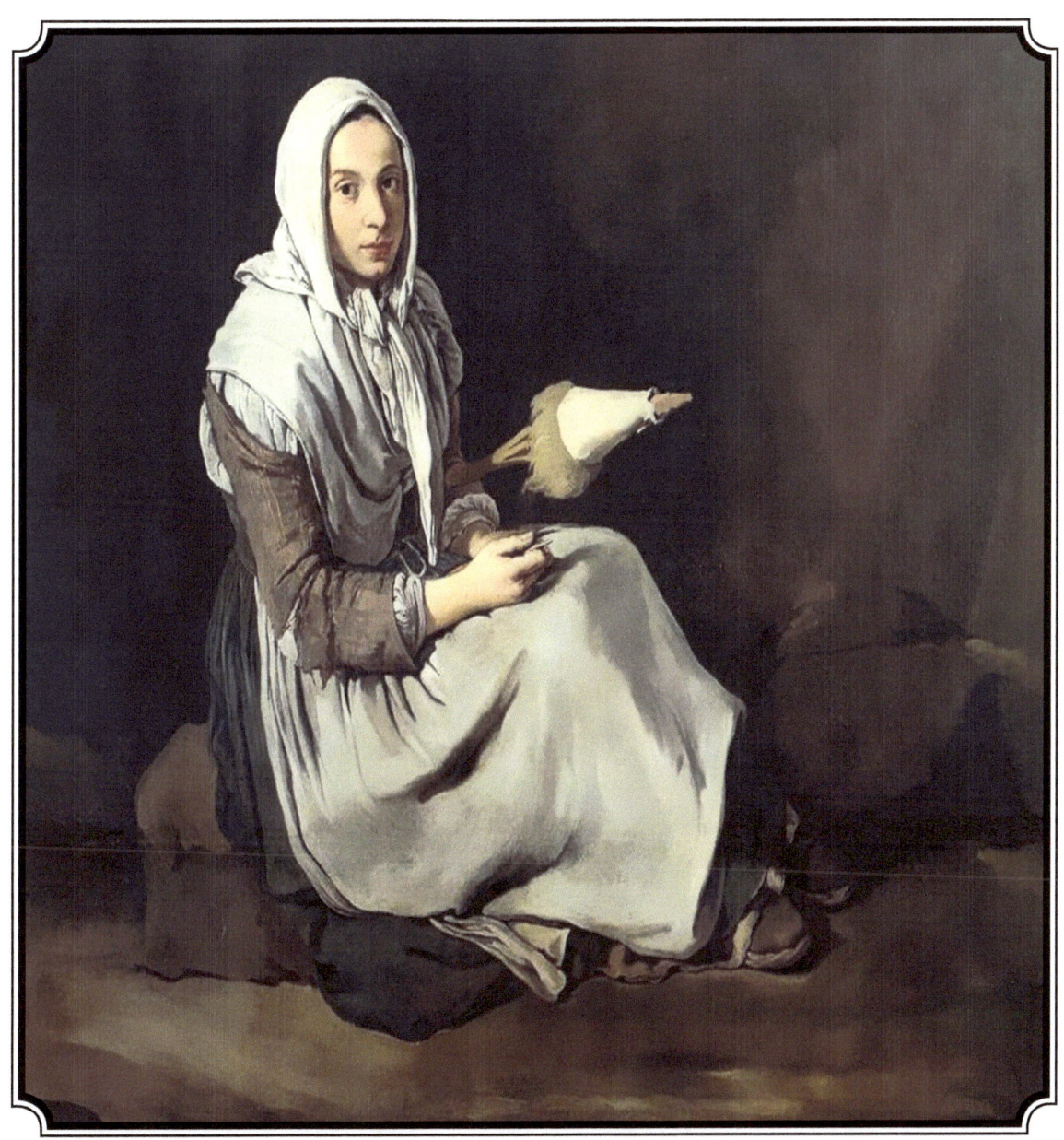

"The Spinster", by Giacomo Ceruti
Oil, 1720

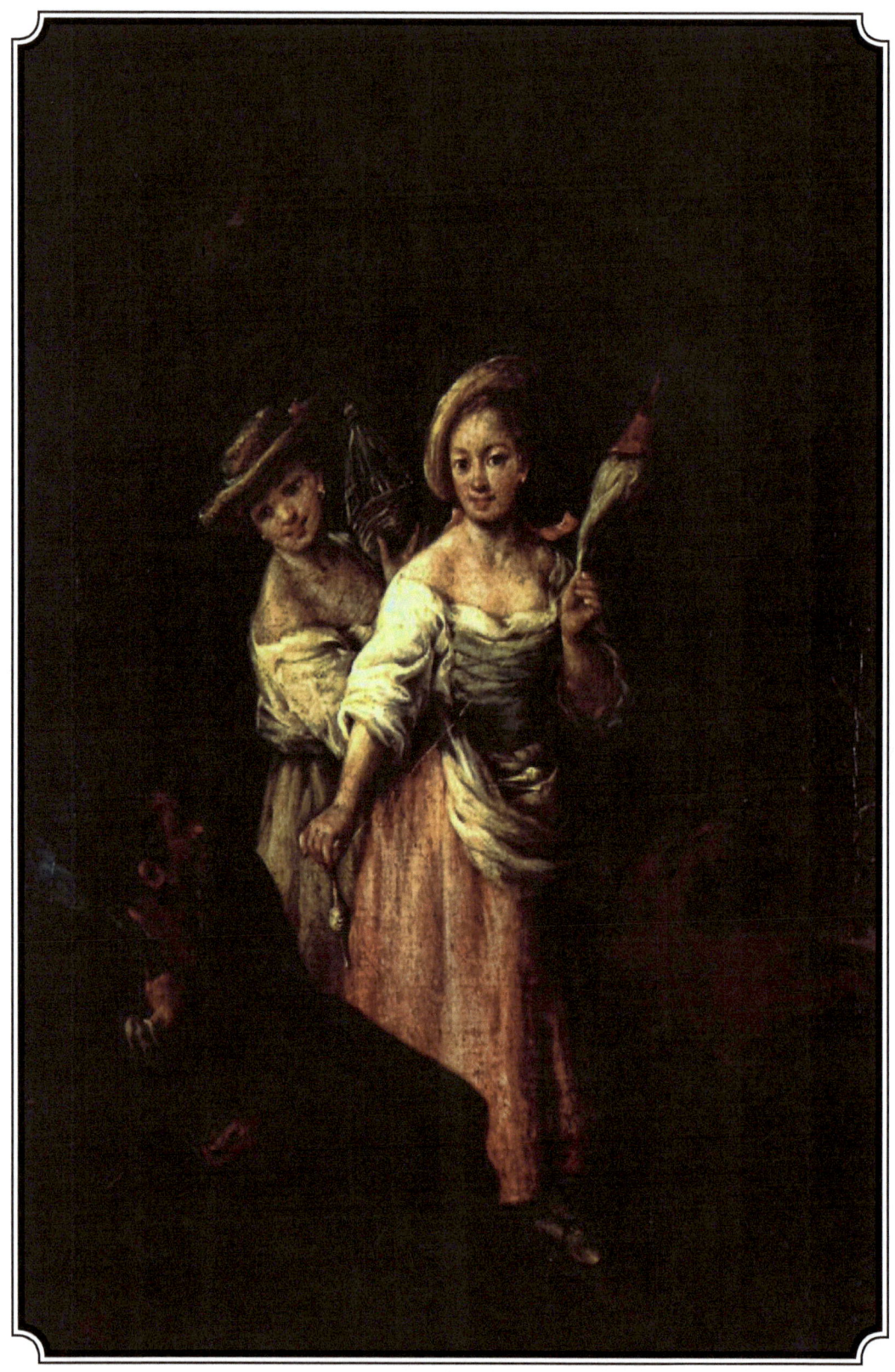

"The Spinsters", by Pietro Longhi
Oil, c.1700s

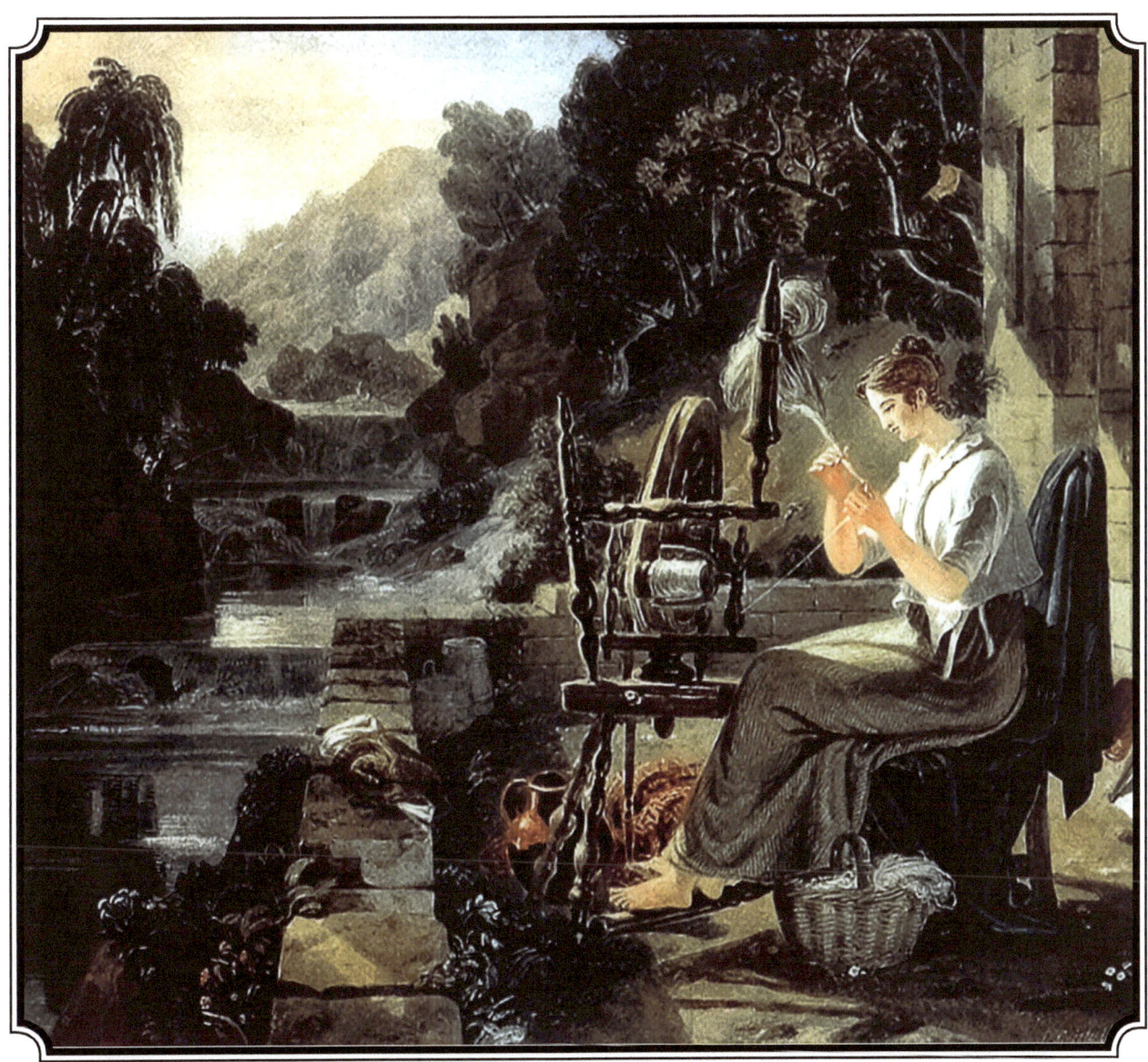

"Bessy and Her Spinning Wheel", by Joshua Cristall
Oil, c.1700s

A spinster is sitting in the garden handspinning fiber from a distaff on a Saxony style spinning wheel.

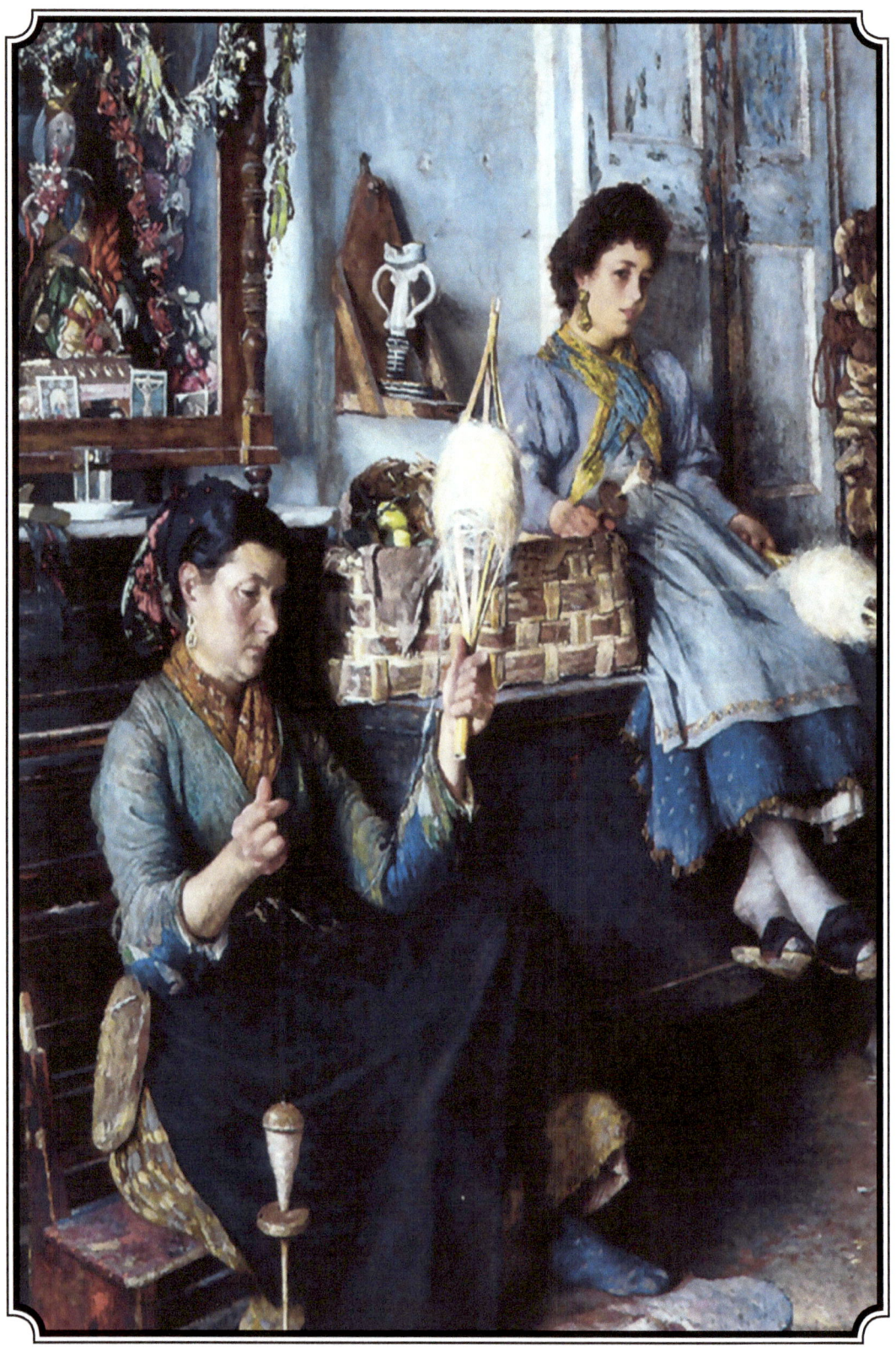

"Venetian Women Spinning Wool", by Marius Michel
Oil, c.1800s

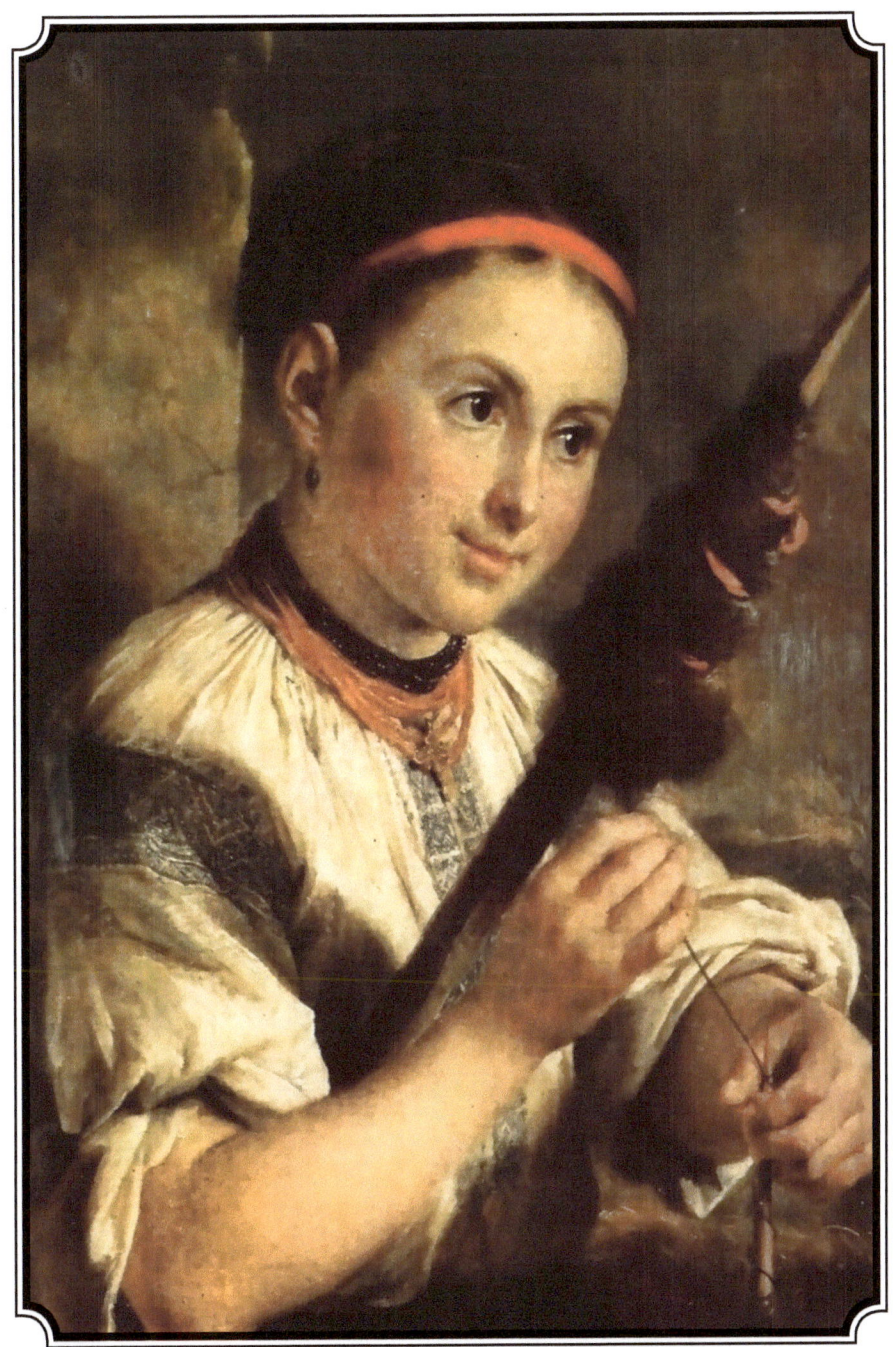

"The Spinster", by Vasily Tropinin
Oil, 1820

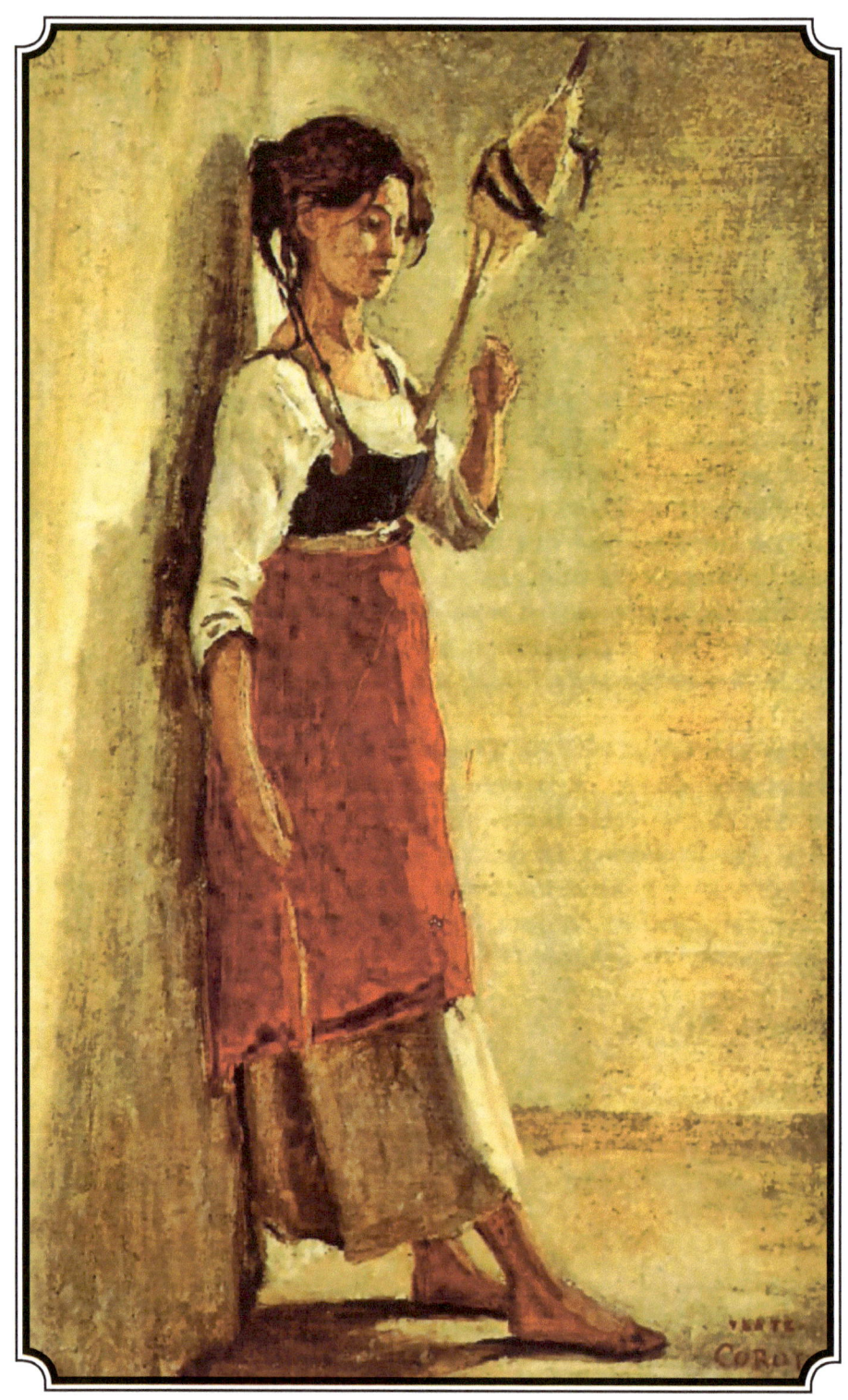

"Young Italian Woman from Papigno with Her Spindle", by Camille Corot
Oil, 1826

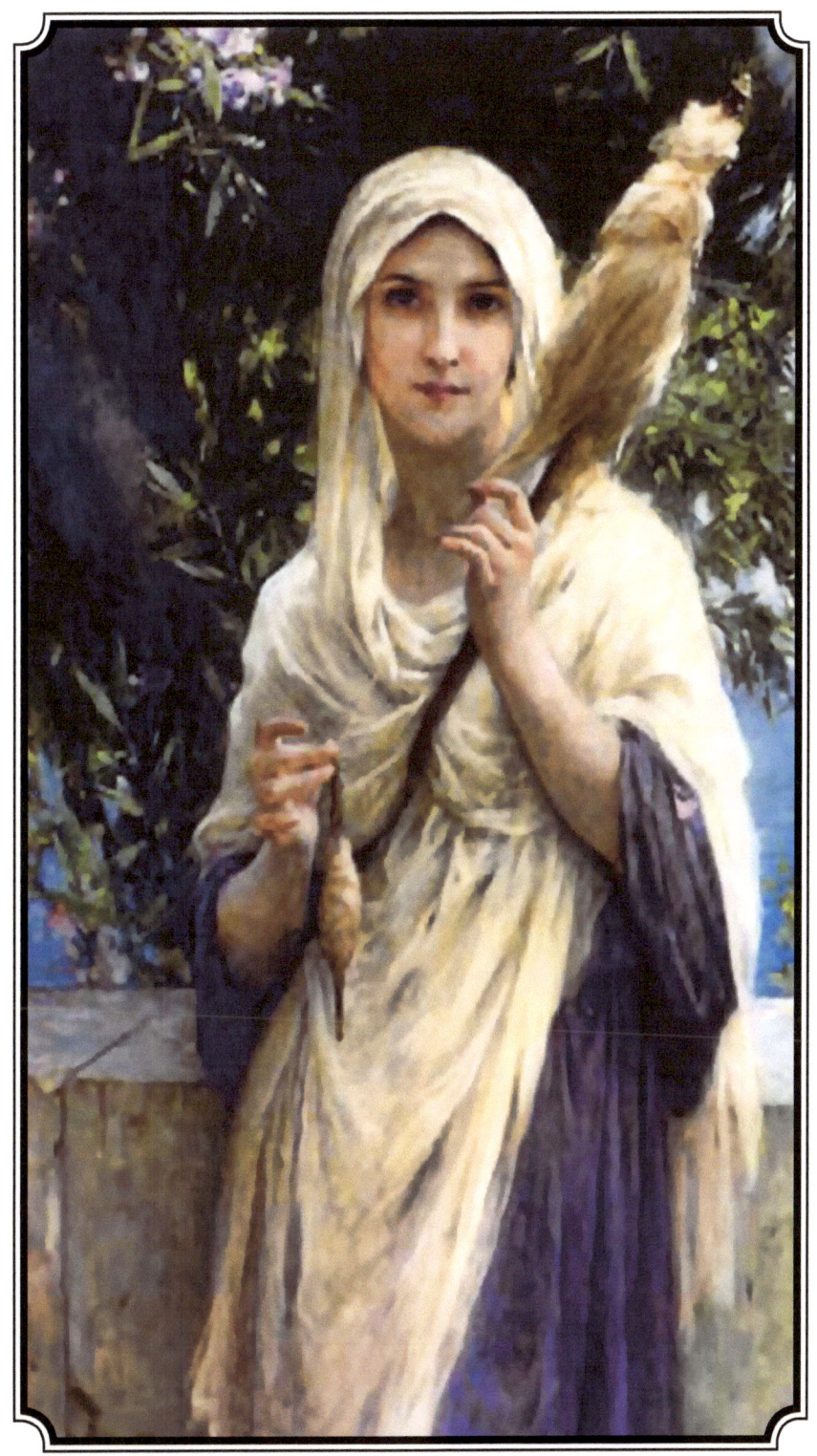

"Spinster by the Sea", by Charles Amable Lenoir
Oil, 1826

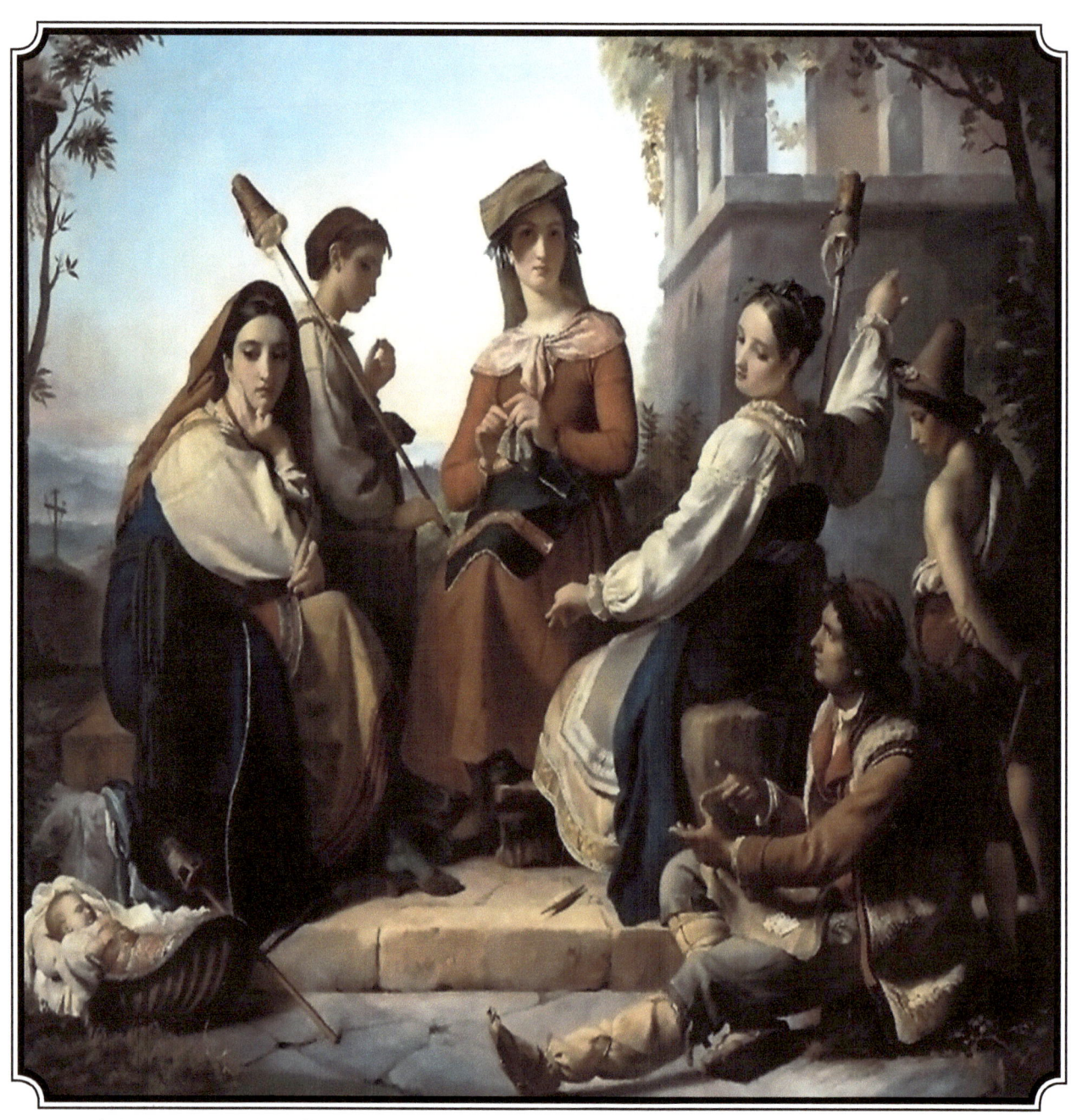

"Women Spinning in Fondi", by François Navez
Oil, 1845

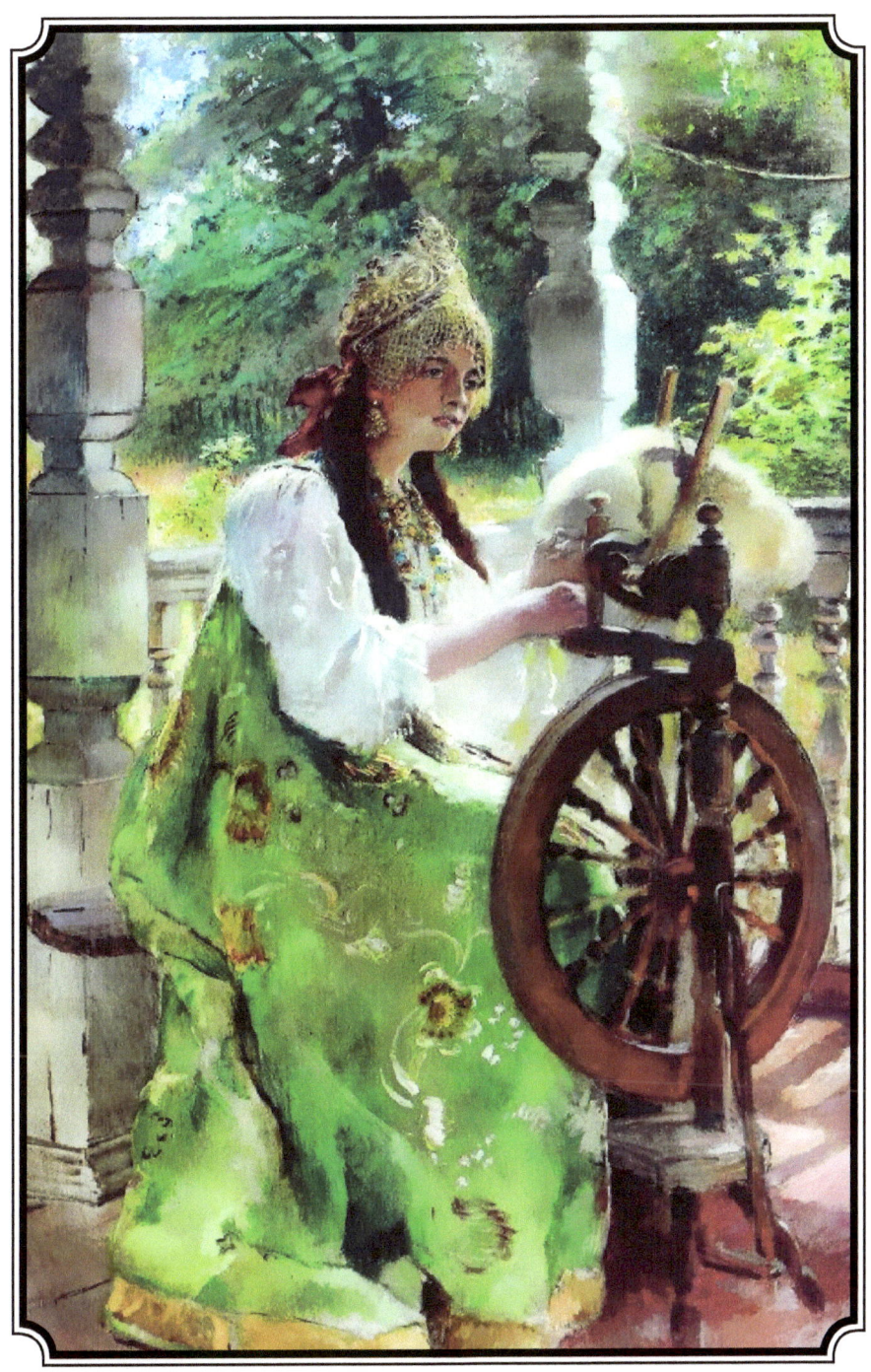

"At the Spinner Wheel", by Konstantin Makovsky
Oil, c.1850s

This painting portrays a spinster using a Castle style spinning wheel. A Castle wheel is stacked vertically with the flyer positioned above the fly wheel.

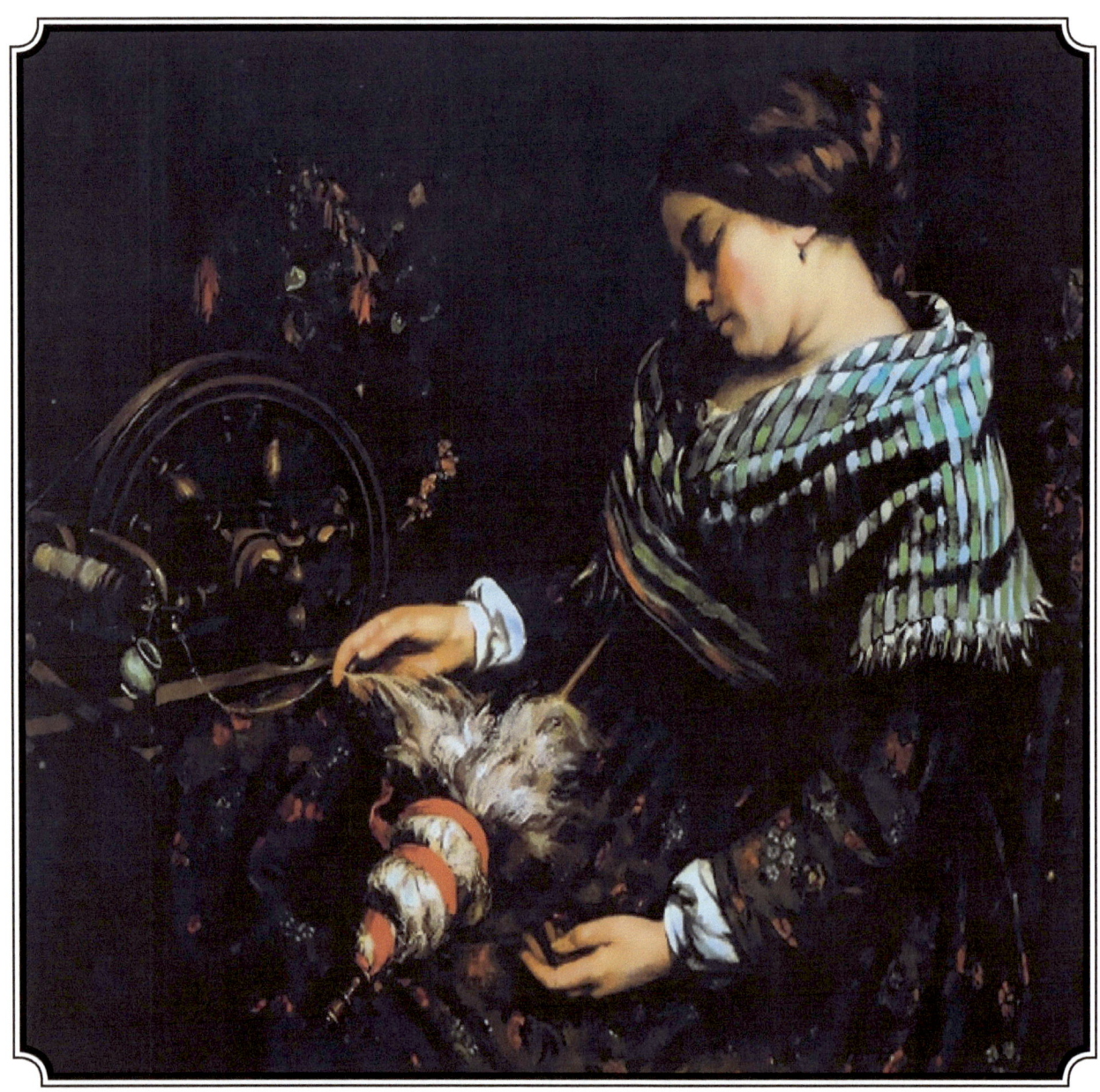

"The Sleeping Spinster," by Gustave Courbet
Oil, 1853

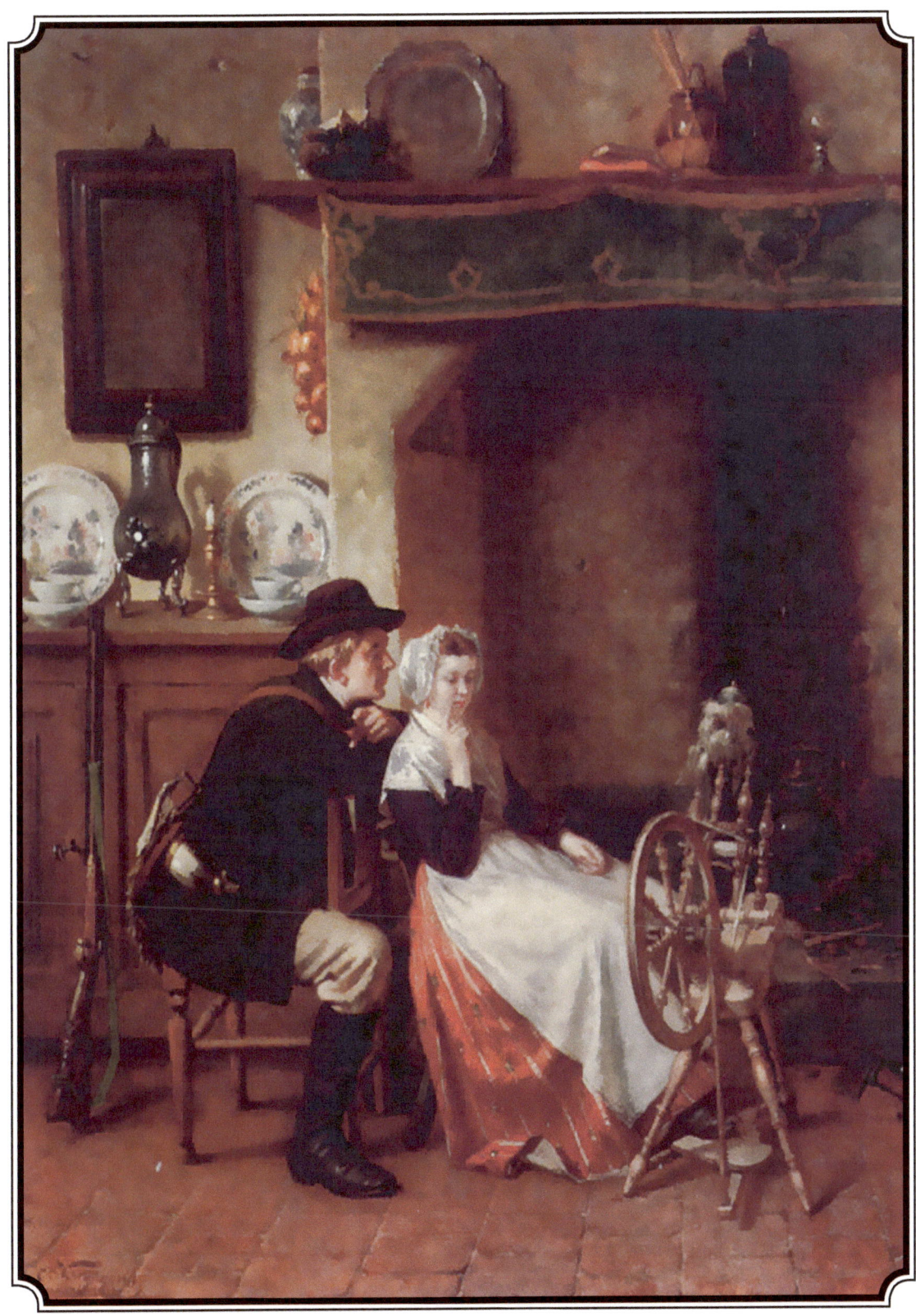

"Spinning a Yarn", by Ch. Van Wingaert
Oil, 1872

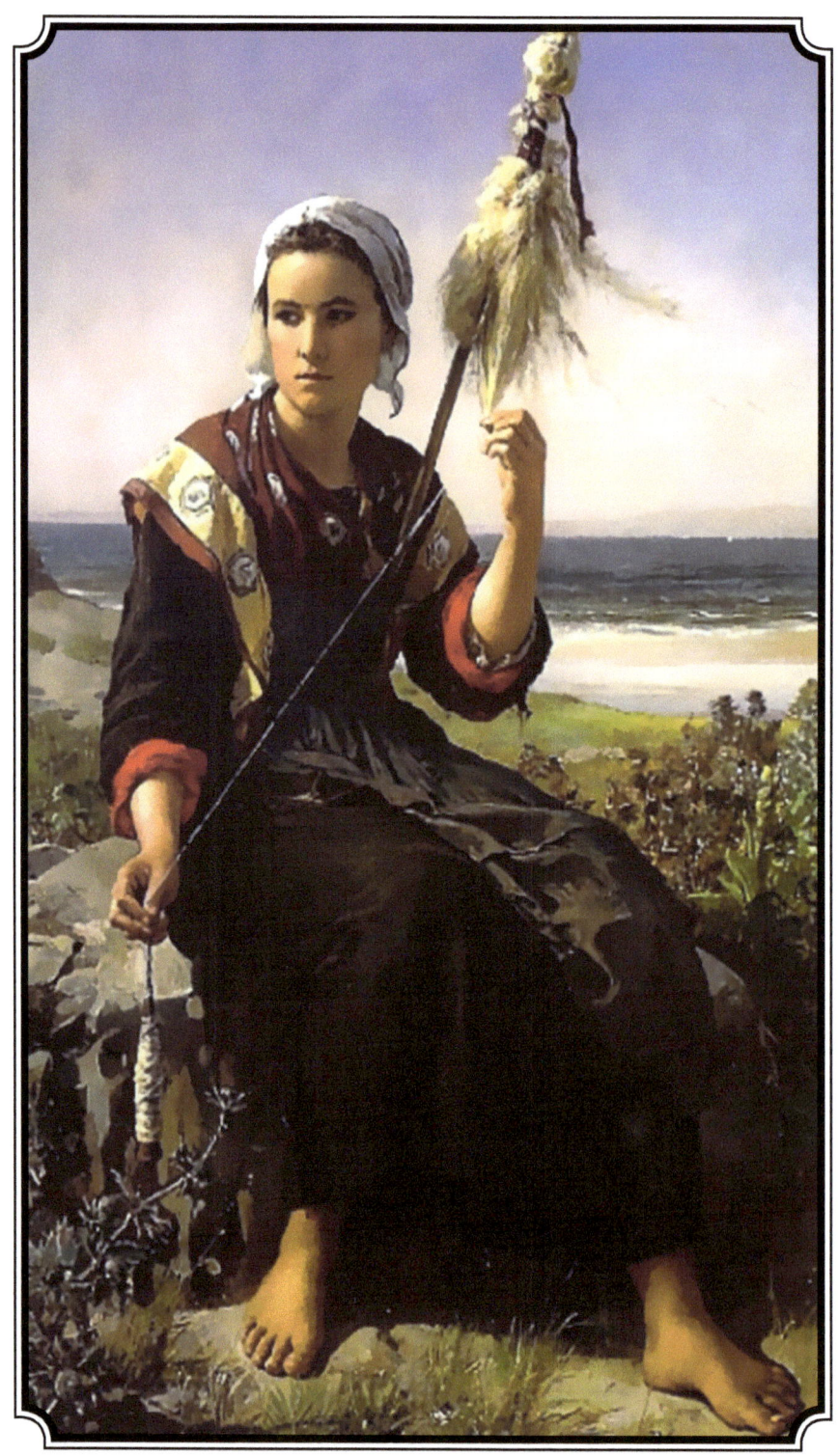

"The Spinster by the Shore", by Jules Breton
Oil, 1872

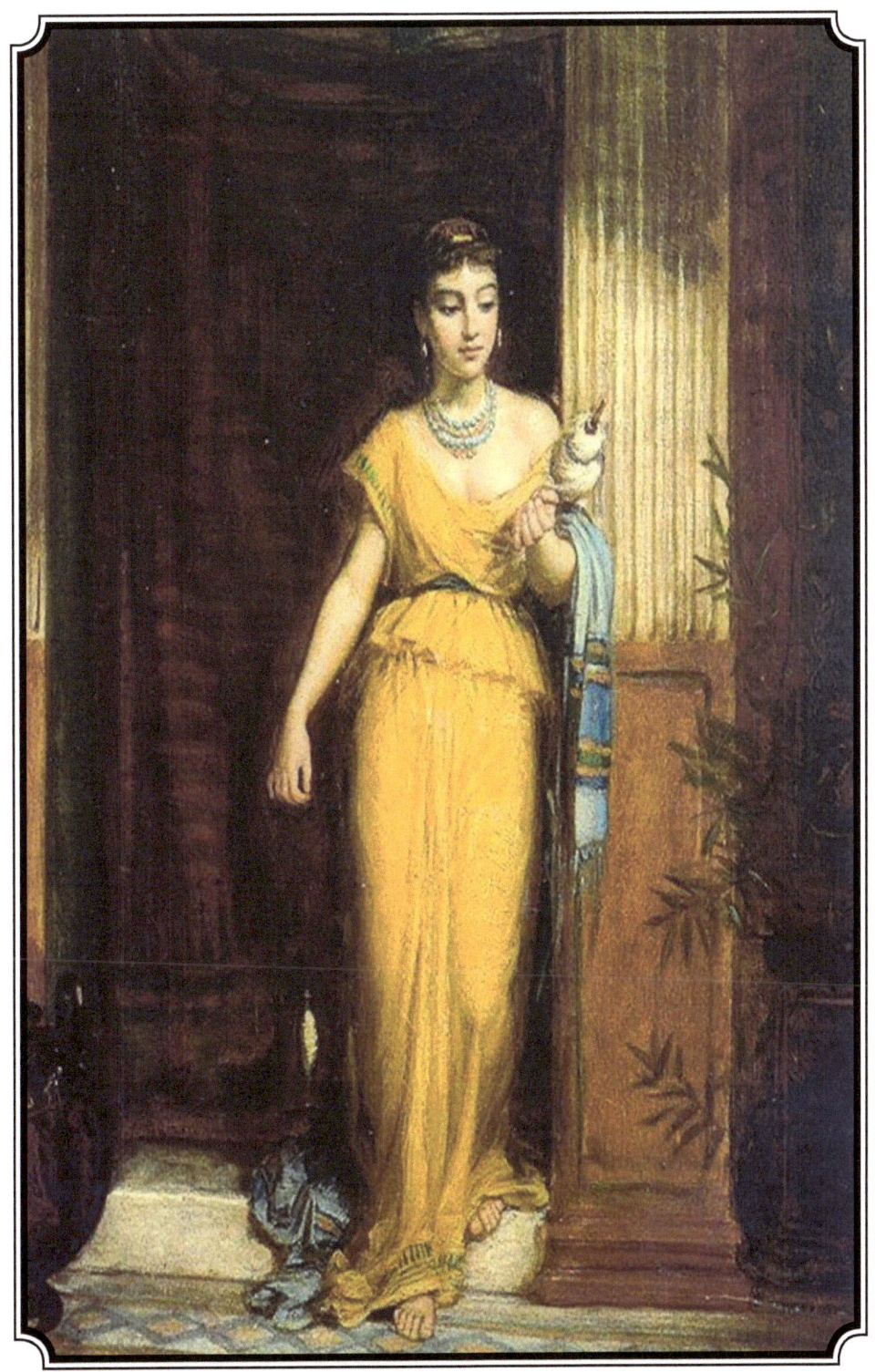

"La Fileuse", by John W. Waterhouse
Oil, 1874

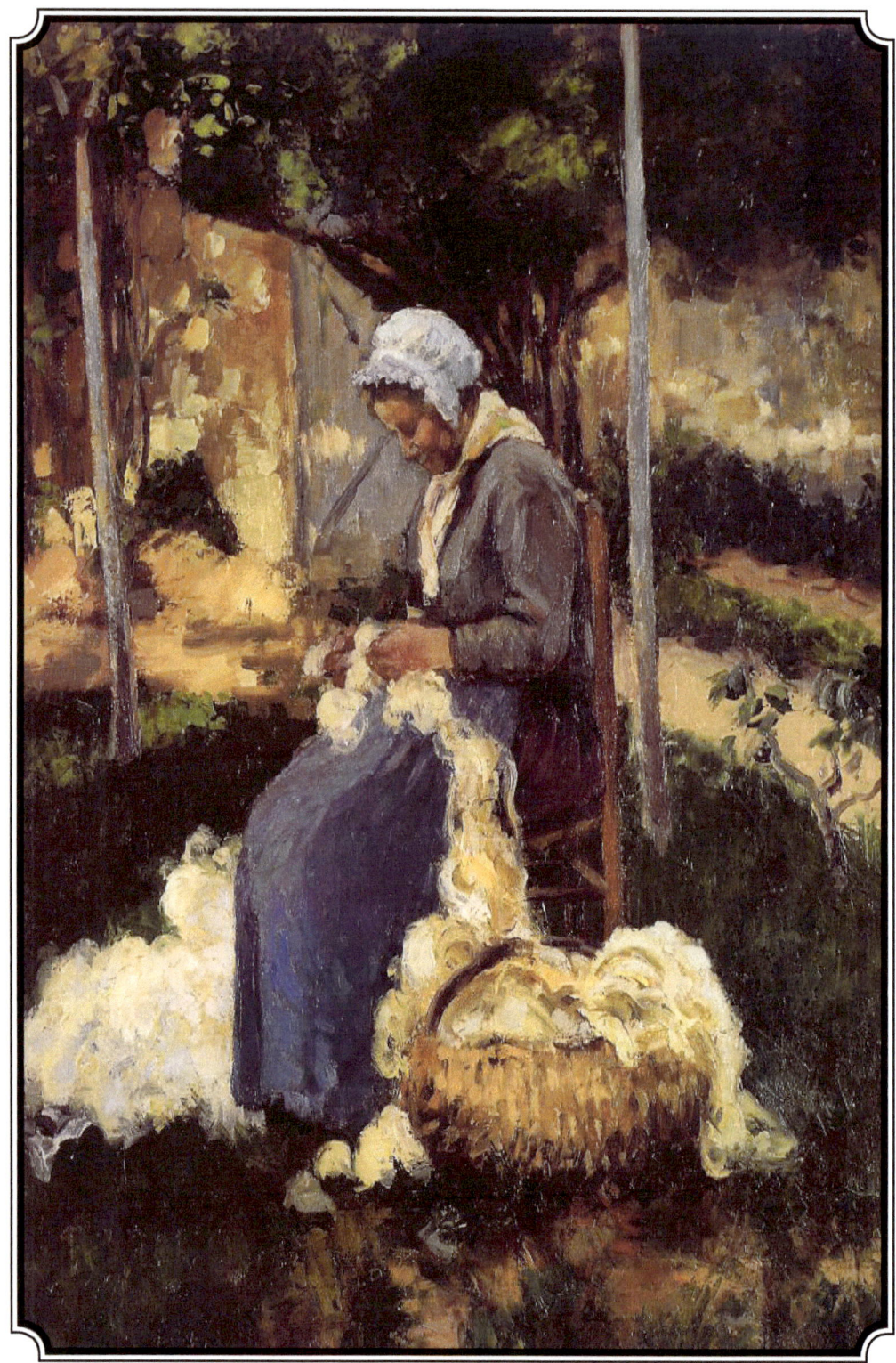

"Female Peasant Carding Wool"
by Camille Pissarro
Oil, 1875

A woman prepares washed fleece, for spinning, by hand carding the fibers. Carding separates and straightens fibers for easy drafting and helps produce a soft lofty yarn.

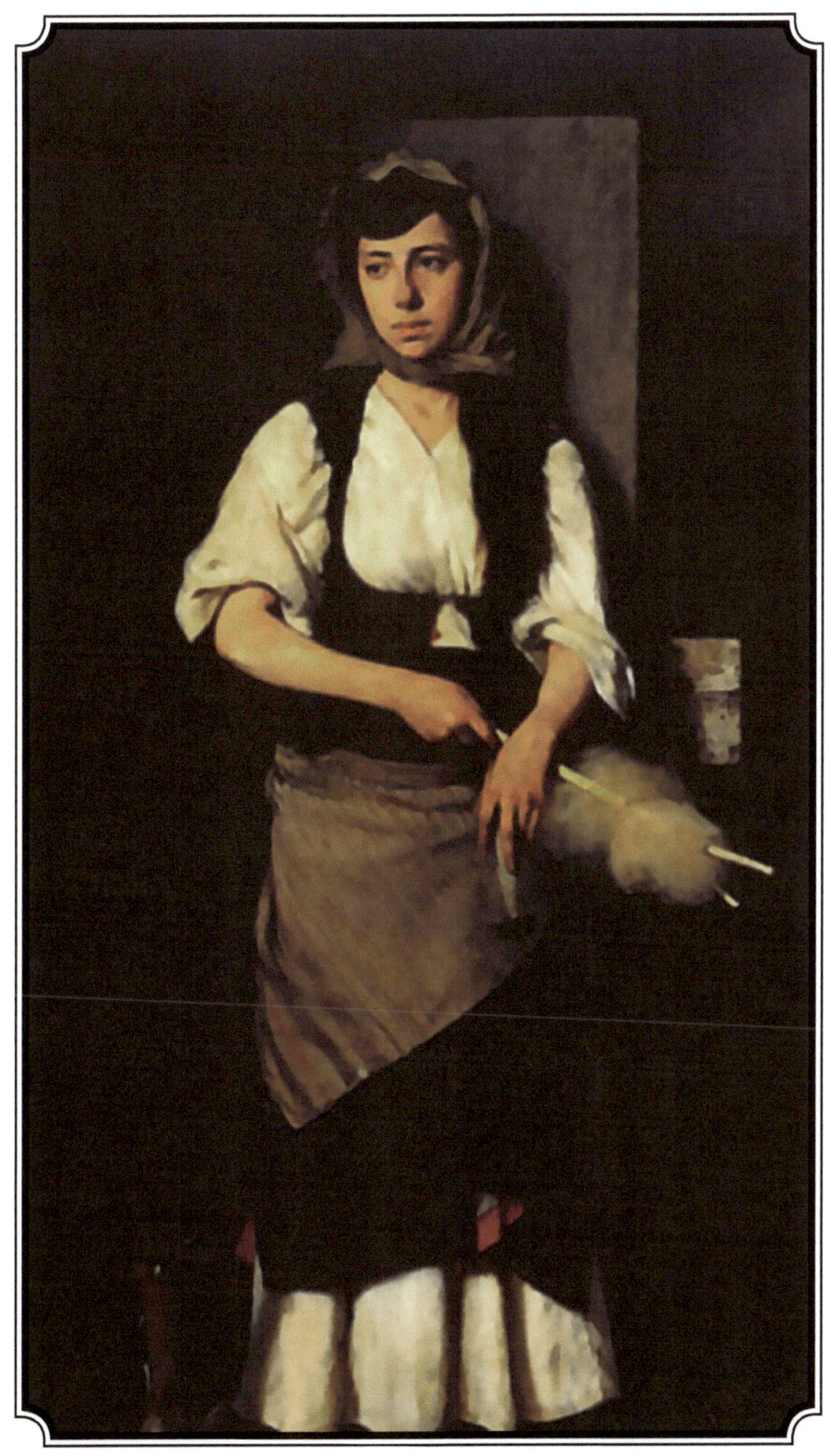

"Girl with a Distaff and a Spindle", by Polychronis Lembesis
Oil, 1876

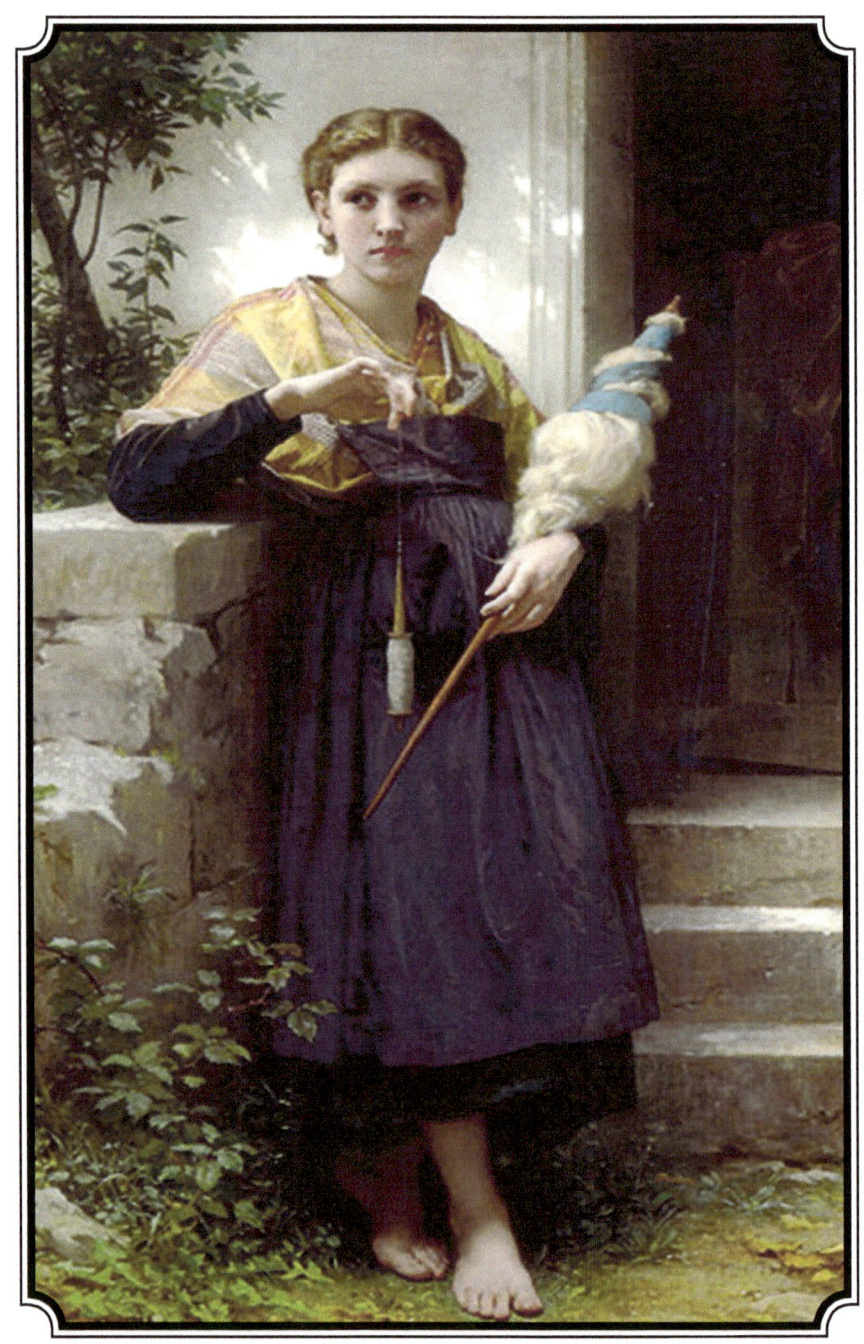

"The Spinner"
by William-Adolphe Bouguereau
Oil, 1884

A young woman is holding a distaff wrapped with fiber and spinning with a drop spindle.

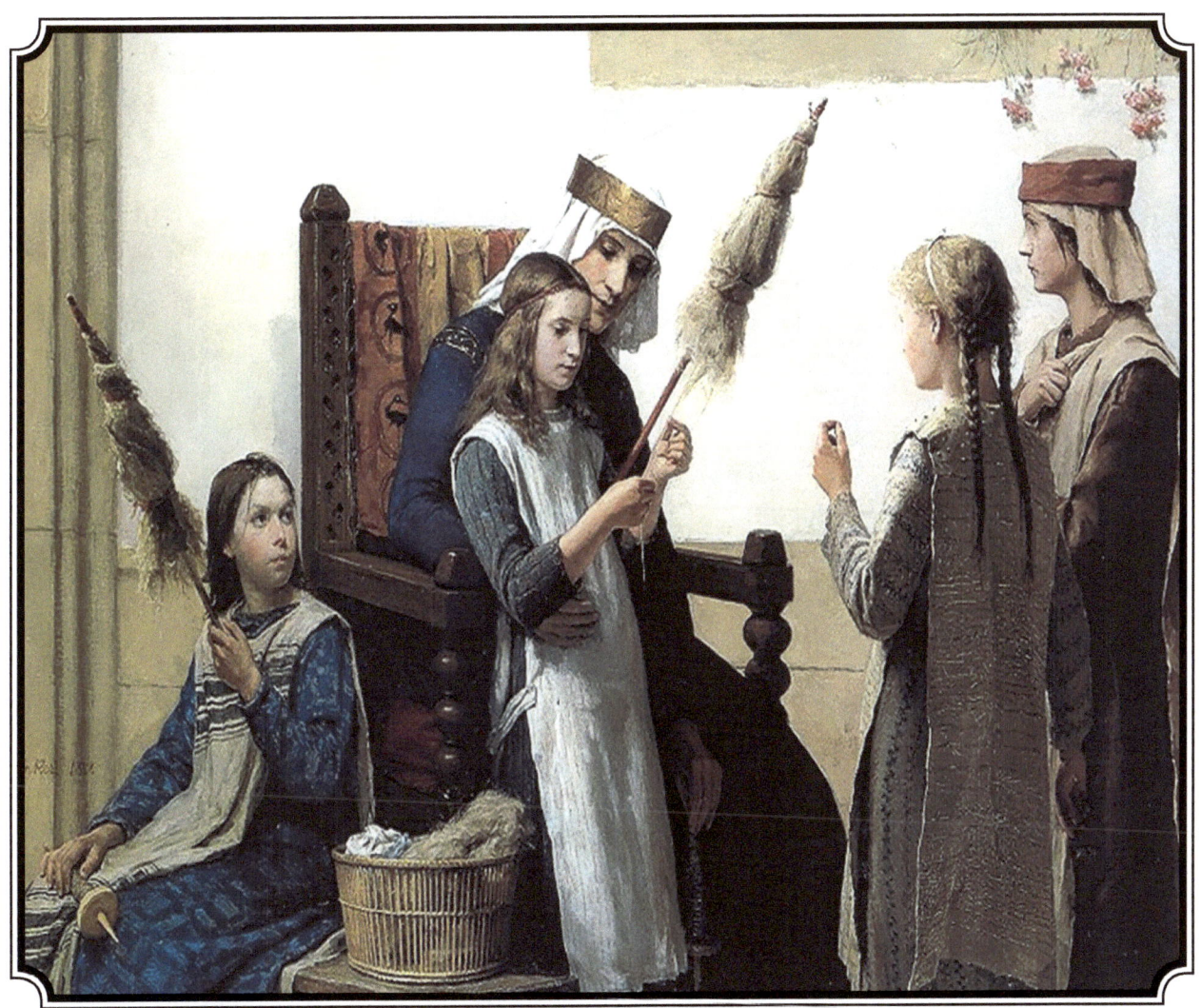

"Queen Bertha and Spinners", by Albert Anker
Oil, 1888

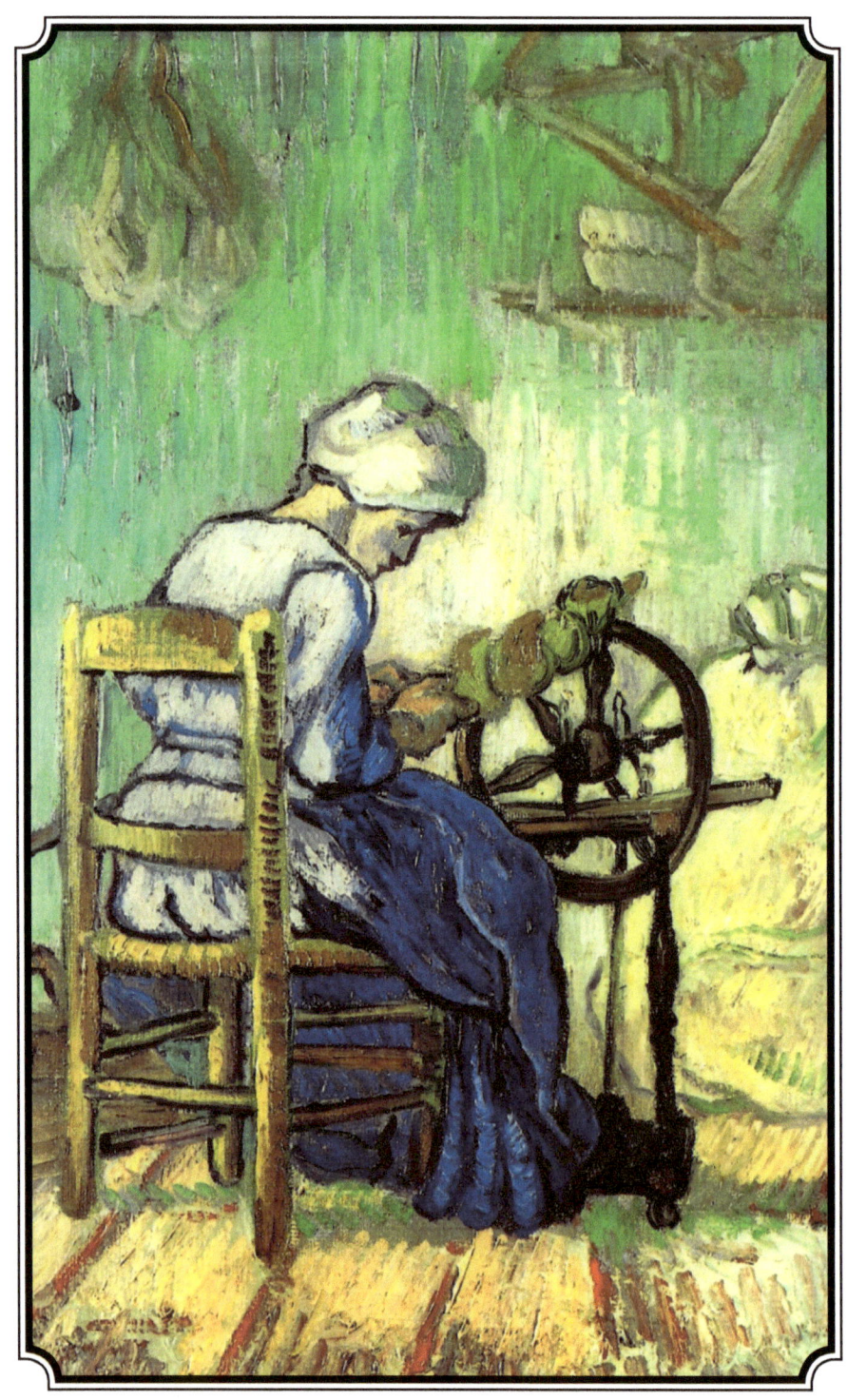

"The Spinster", by Vincent Van Gogh
Oil, 1889

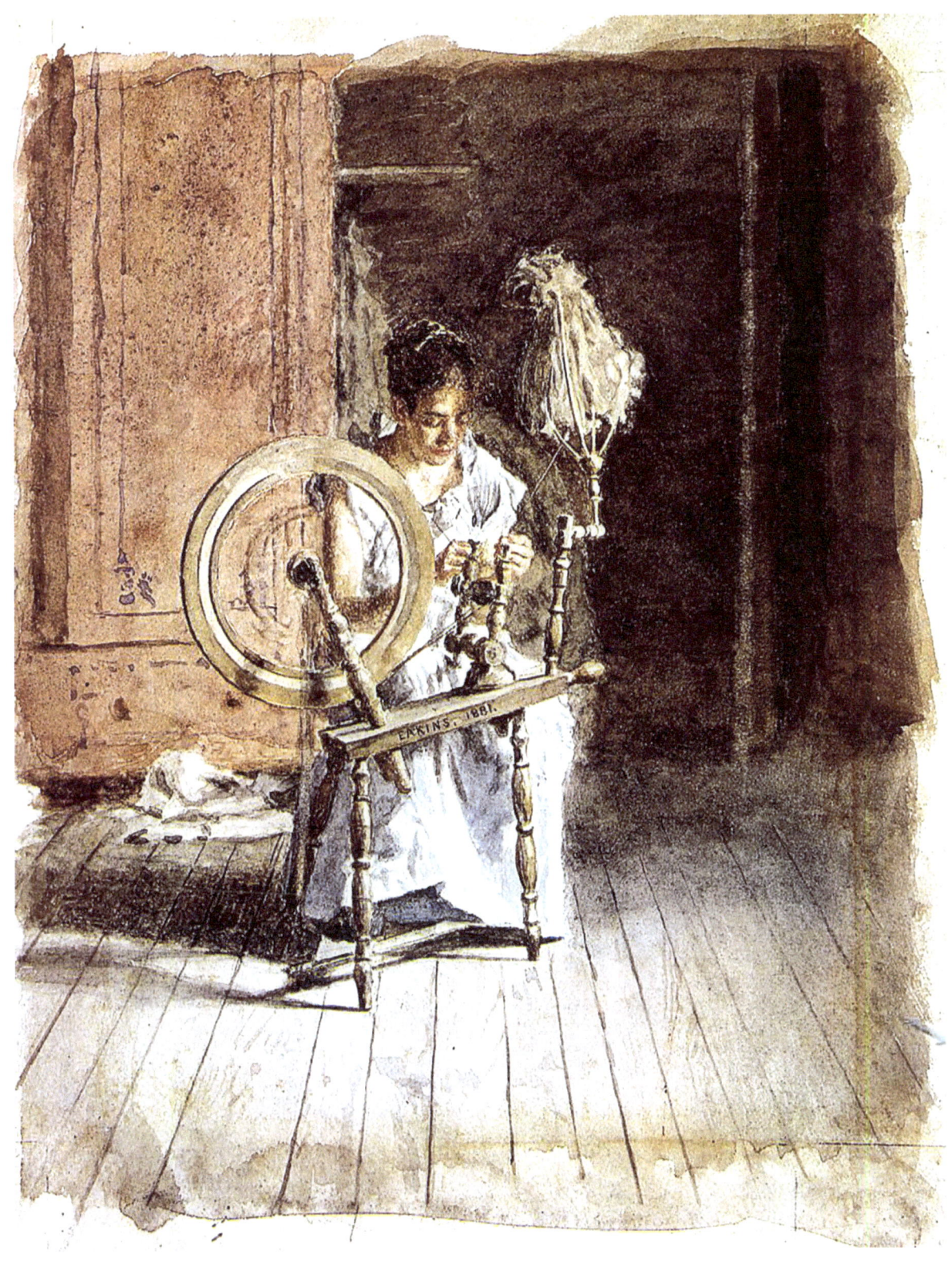

"Spinning", by Thomas Eakins
Watercolor, 1881

Drawings & Prints

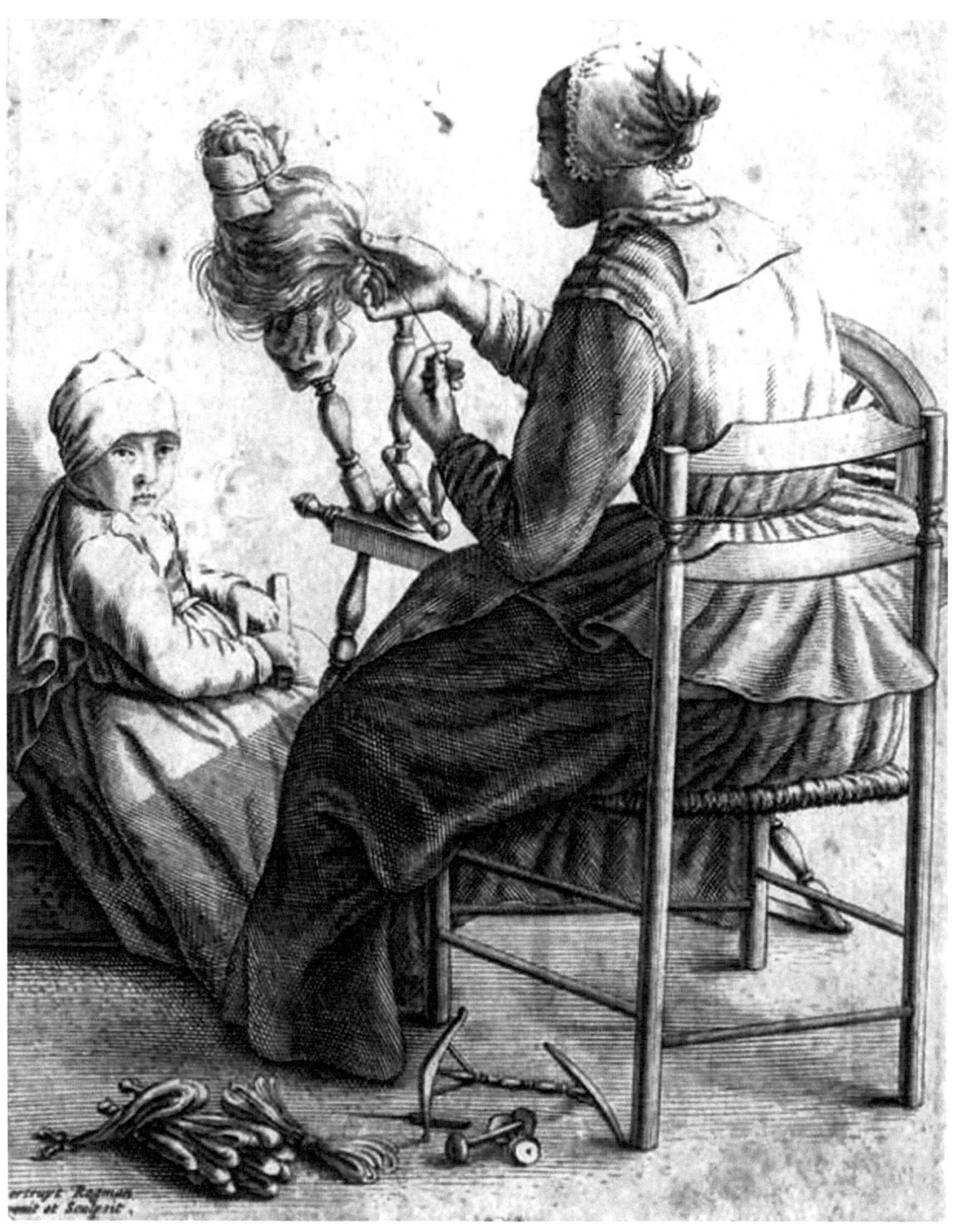

"The Spinster", by Geertruydt Roghman
Print, 1600-1650

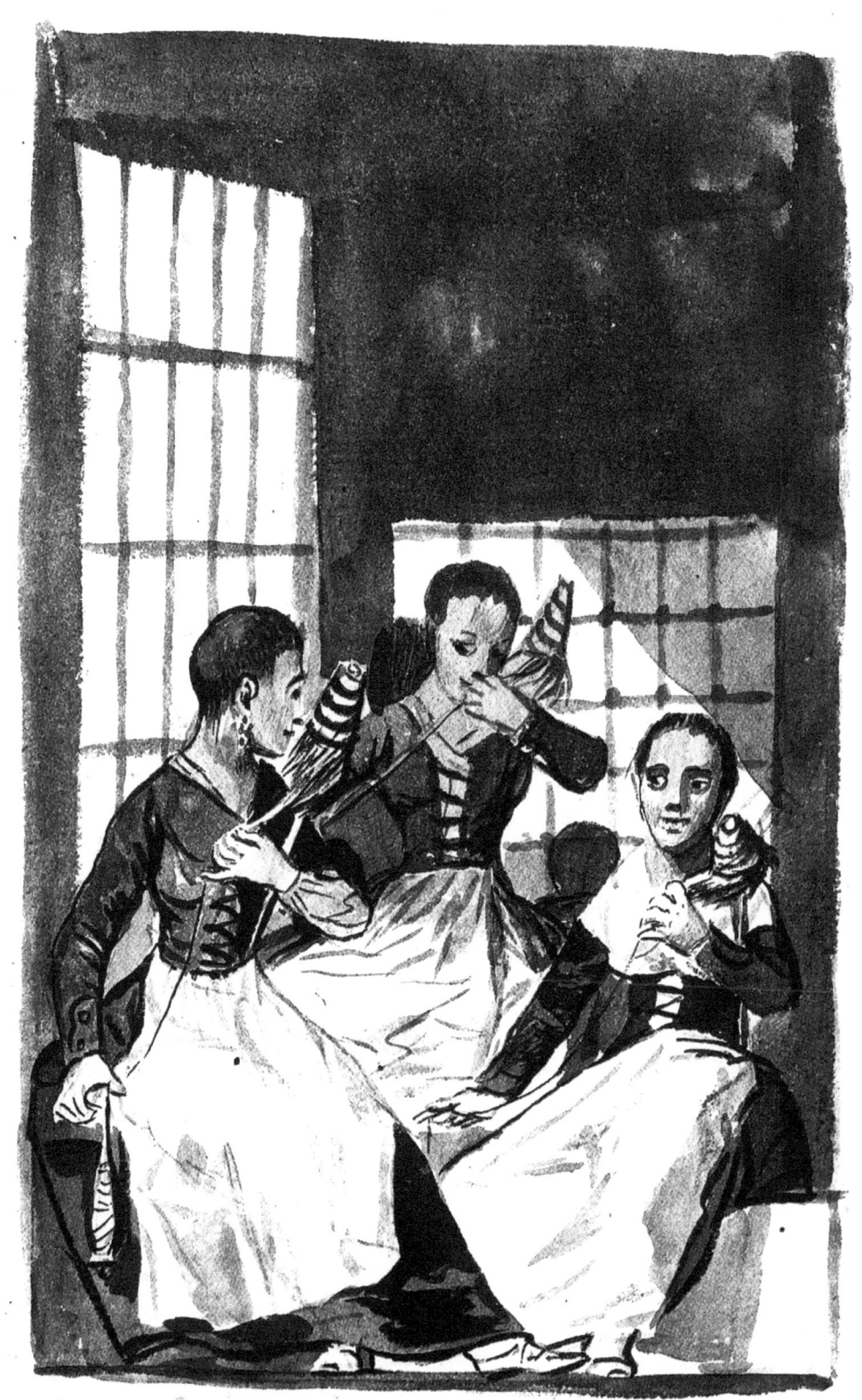

"How they Spin", by Francisco De Goya
Ink wash, c.1789

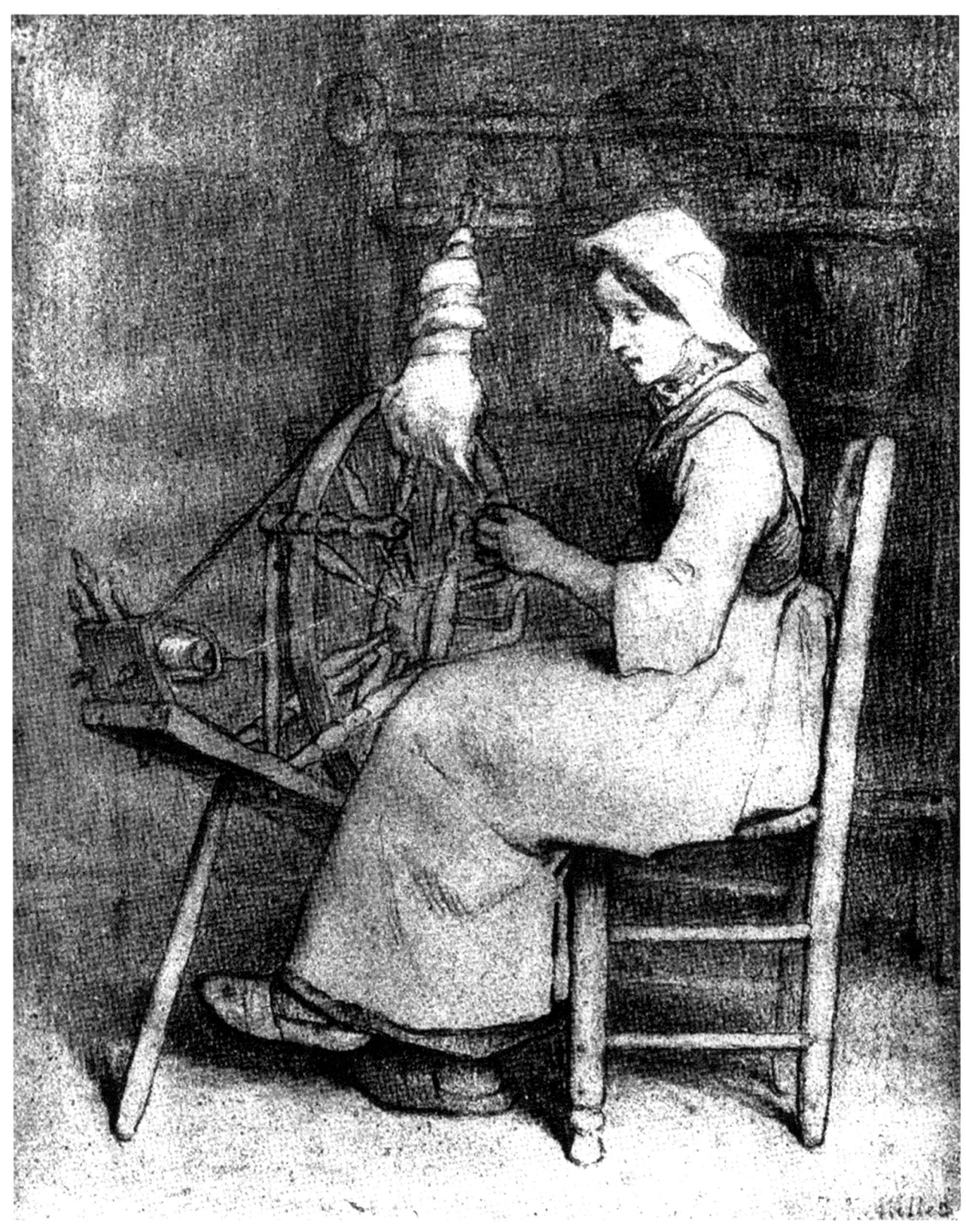

"The Spinster, by Jean-Francois Millet
Charcoal drawing, 1850s

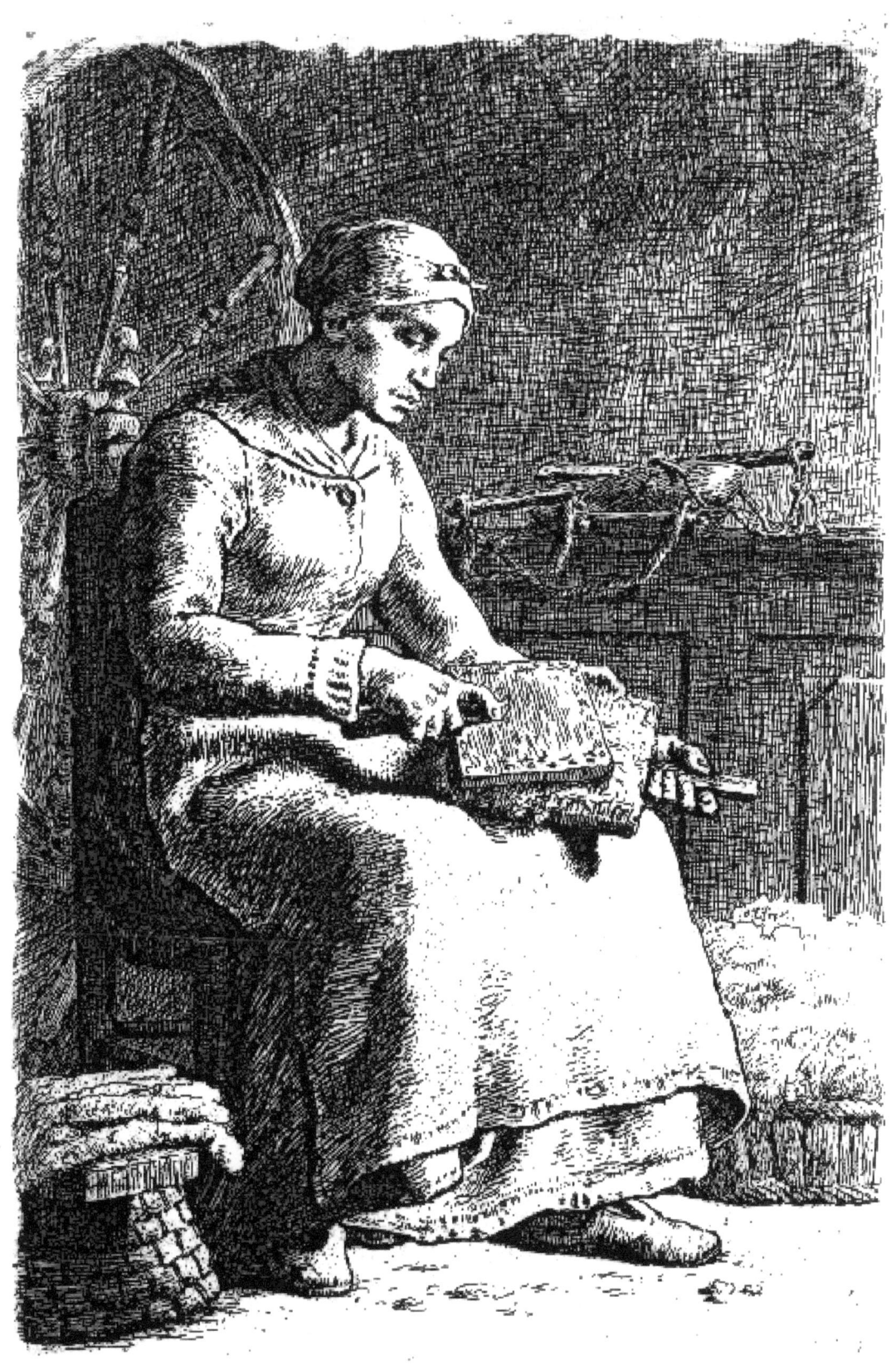

"Woman Carding Wool", by Jean-Francois Millet
Print, 1850s

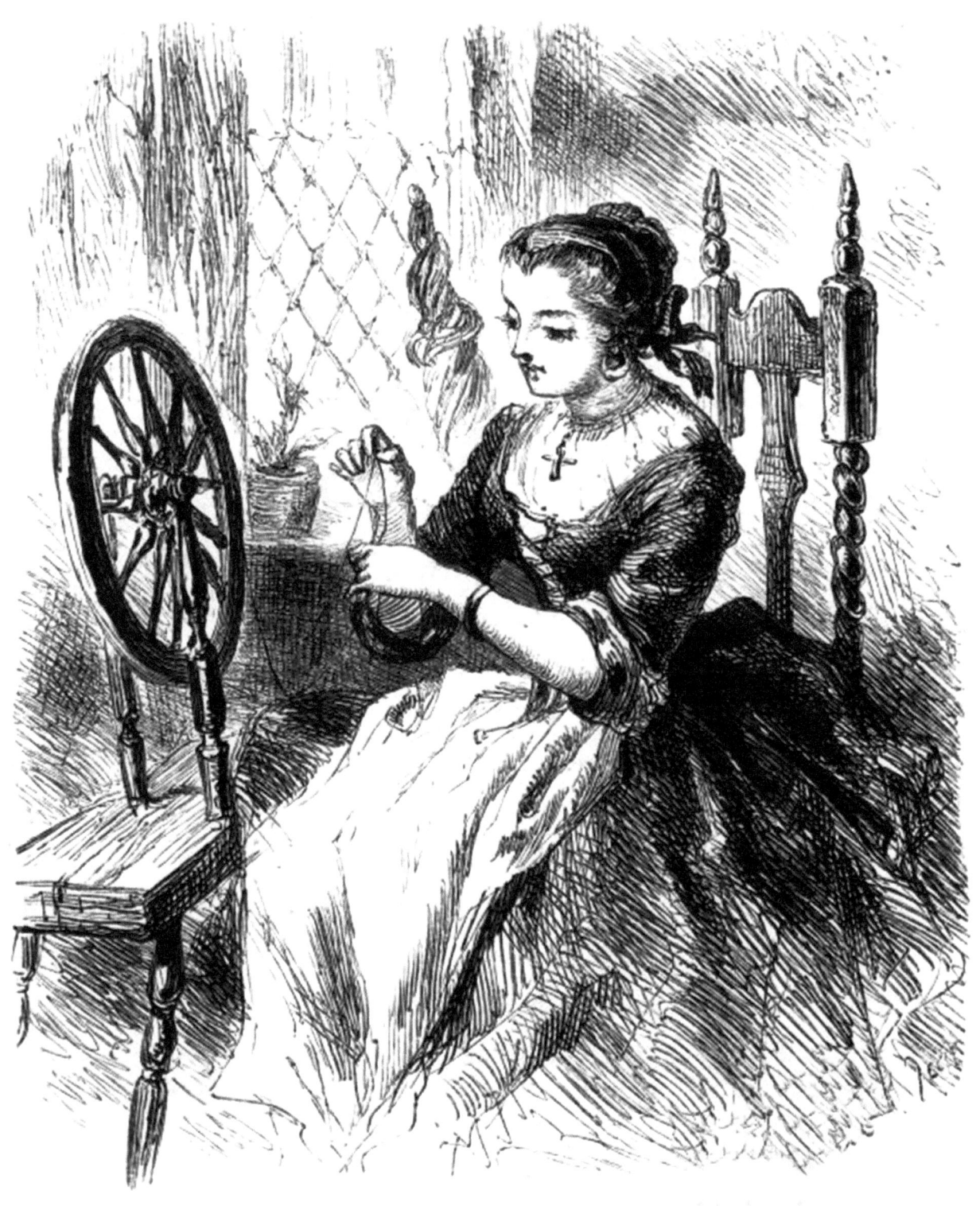

"Katrina at the Spinning Wheel", by Felix Darley
Print, 1864

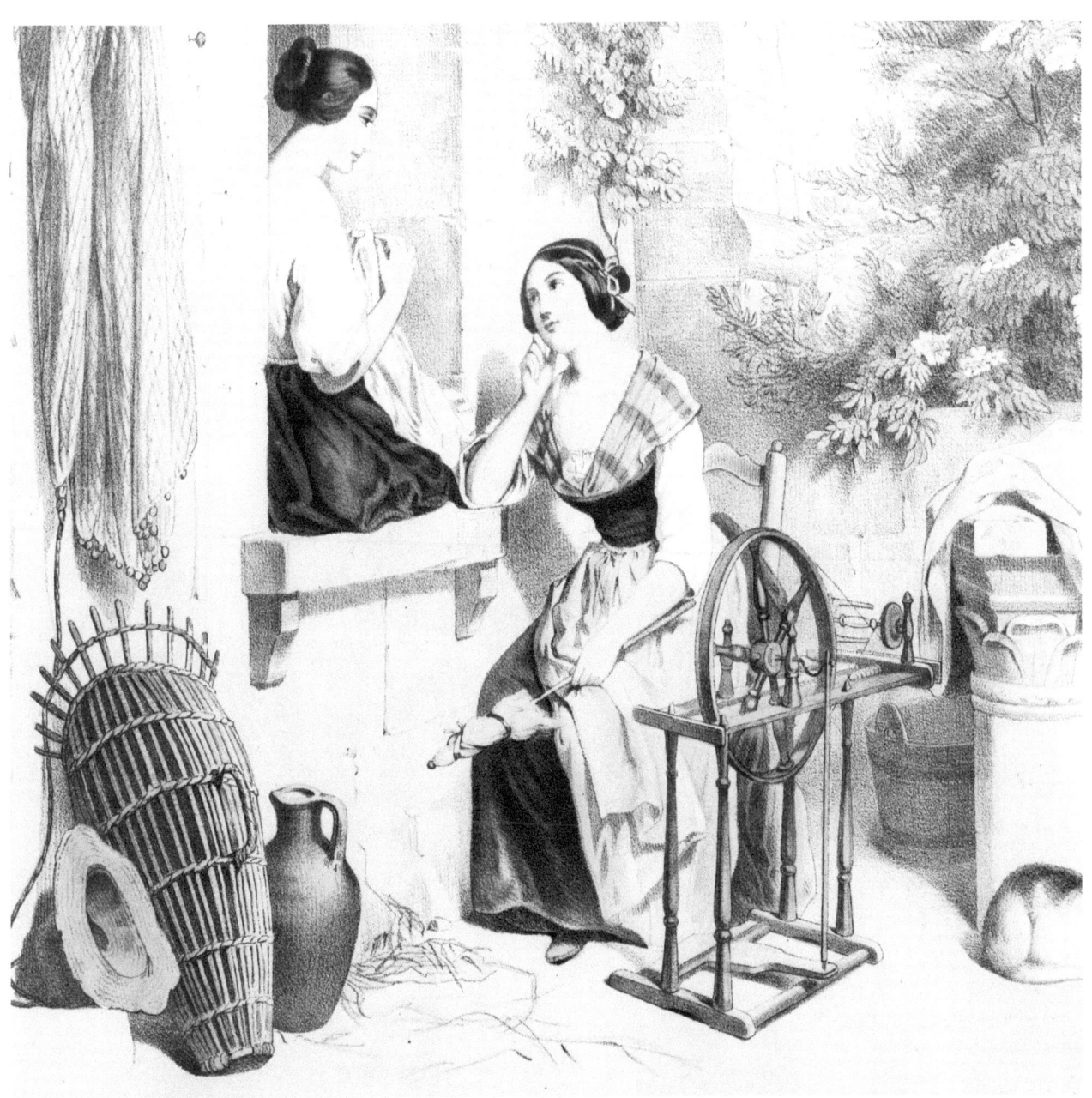

"The Spinsters", by Jules Breton
Print, 1872

This print engraving portrays a woman spinning with a Norwegian style spinning wheel. The Norwegian wheel looks similar to the Saxony wheel. It has a large wheel, four legs, and a horizontal bench.

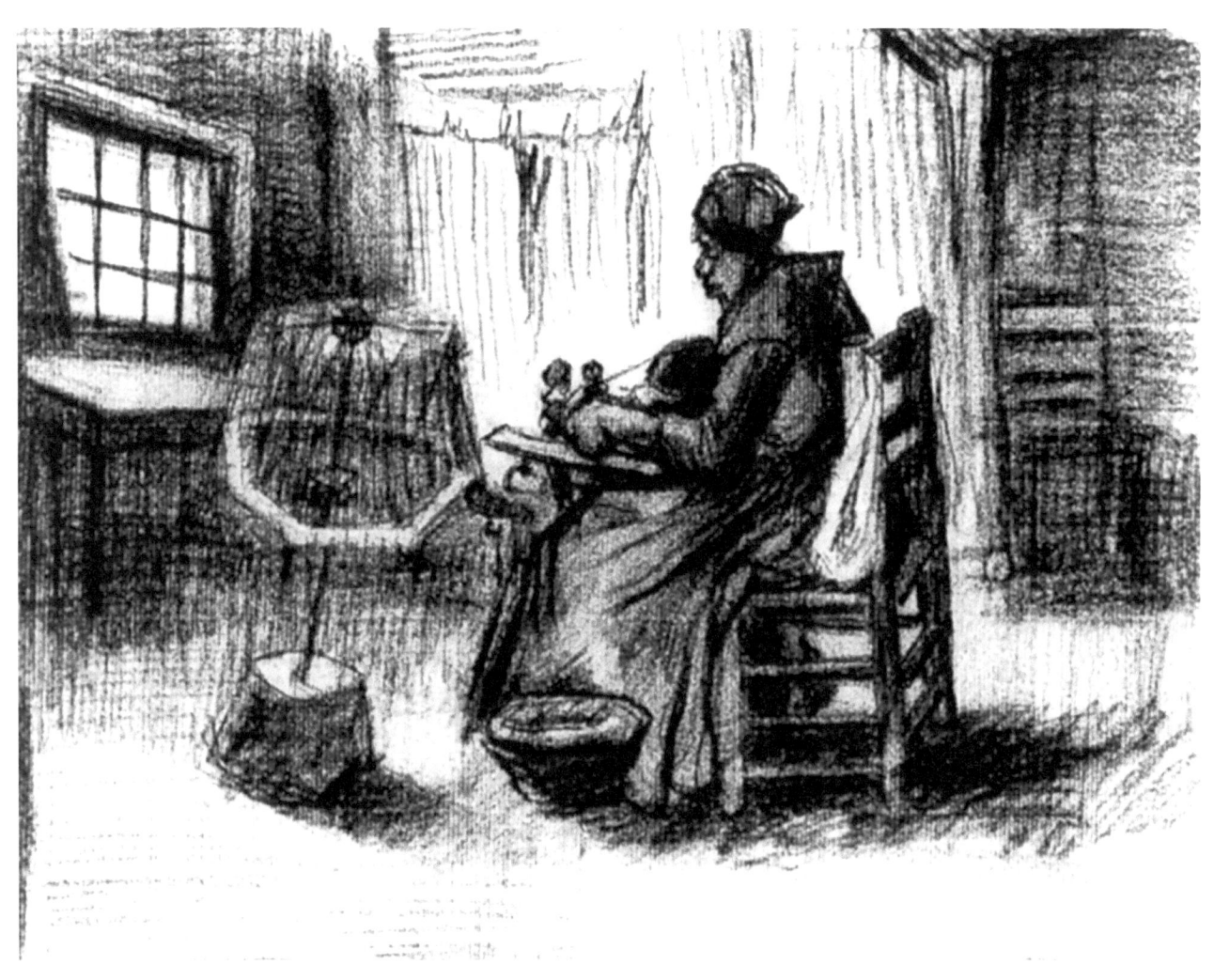

"The Spinster", by Vincent Van Gogh
Charcoal drawing, 1884

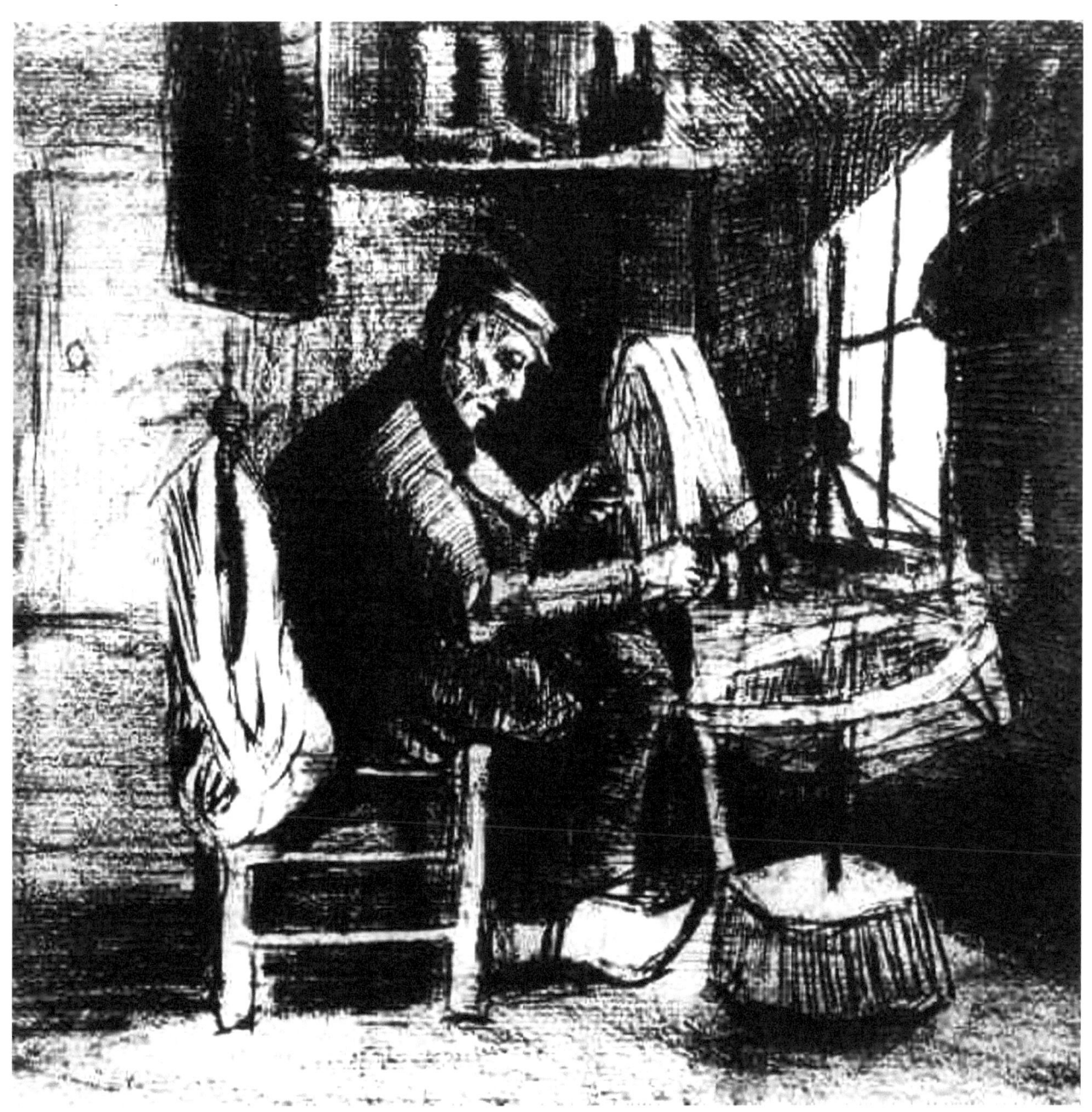

"A Spinner Reeling Yarn from a Spinning Wheel", by Vincent Van Gogh
Charcoal drawing, 1889

Reeling the spun yarn onto an "umbrella style" swift was another method used to remove the yarn from the spinning wheel and to form a skein of yarn.

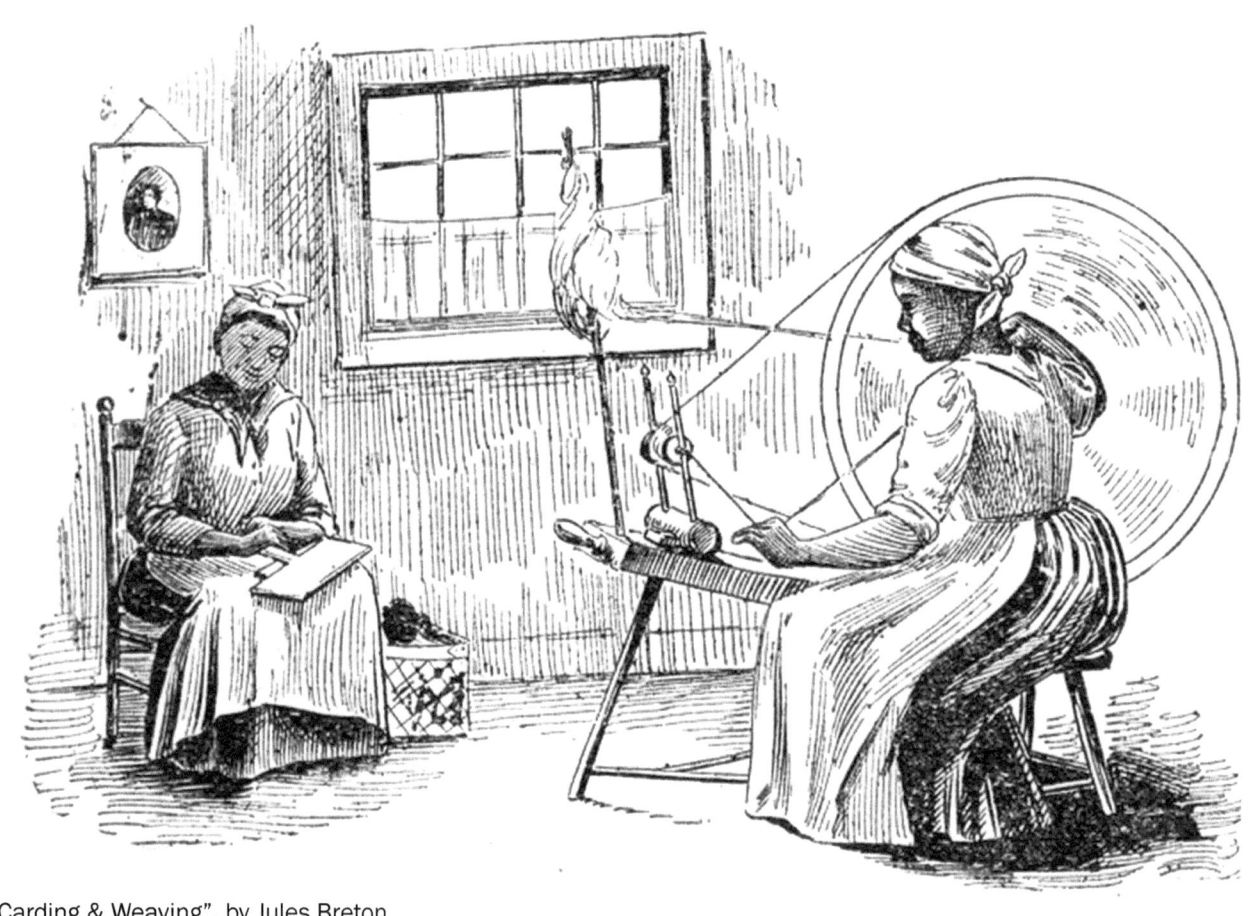

"Carding & Weaving", by Jules Breton
Print, 1889

About the Author

Tulasi Zimmer is an award winning handspinner, professional artist, and educator. She art career expands into the fields of painting and drawing, graphic design, web design, multimedia production, and fiber arts. In 1999, Tulasi created the award winning website The Joy of Hand-spinning (JOH). JOH provides useful information, free video demonstrations, and publishes instructional materials that will enable anyone to learn how to handspin natural fibers into yarn with a drop spindle and/or spinning wheel. The JOH web site continues to be a popular resource on the topic of handspinning. Visit www.joyofhandspinning.com